OTHER BOOKS BY ERIC FONER

Free Soil, Free Labor, Free Men:
The Ideology of the Republican Party Before the Civil War (1970)

America's Black Past:
A Reader in Afro-American History (editor, 1971)

Nat Turner (editor, 1971)

Tom Paine and Revolutionary America (1976)

Politics and Ideology in the Age of the Civil War (1980)

Nothing But Freedom: Emancipation and Its Legacy (1983)

Reconstruction: America's Unfinished Revolution, 1863–1877 (1988)

A Short History of Reconstruction (1990)

A House Divided: America in the Age of Lincoln
(with Olivia Mahoney, 1990)

The New American History (editor, 1990; rev. ed. 1997)

The Reader's Companion to American History
(editor, with John A. Garraty, 1991)

Freedom's Lawmakers: A Directory of Black Reconstruction Officeholders
(1993; rev. ed. 1996)

Thomas Paine (editor, 1995)

America's Reconstruction: People and Politics after the Civil War
(with Olivia Mahoney, 1995)

The Story of American Freedom (1998)

WHO OWNS HISTORY?

WHO OWNS HISTORY?

RETHINKING THE PAST IN

A CHANGING WORLD

ERIC FONER

ⓗ HILL AND WANG

A DIVISION OF FARRAR, STRAUS AND GIROUX

NEW YORK

Hill and Wang
A division of Farrar, Straus and Giroux
18 West 18th Street, New York 10011

Copyright © 2002 by Eric Foner

Printed in the United States of America
Published in 2002 by Hill and Wang
First paperback edition, 2003

The Library of Congress has cataloged the hardcover edition as follows:
Foner, Eric.
    Who owns history? : rethinking the past in a changing world / Eric Foner.—
1st ed.
        p.   cm.
    Includes bibliographical references and index.
    ISBN-13: 978-0-8090-9704-3 (hc : alk. paper)
    ISBN-10: 0-8090-9704-4 (hc : alk. paper)
        1. United States—History—Philosophy.   2. United States—
Historiography.   3. United States—Politics and government—Philosophy.
I. Title.

E175.9 .F66 2002
973'.01—dc21

                                                                    2001051463

Paperback ISBN-13: 978-0-8090-9705-0
Paperback ISBN-10: 0-8090-9705-2

Designed by Jonathan D. Lippincott

www.fsgbooks.com

P1

FOR ARTHUR WANG

CONTENTS

PREFACE

H istory," writes James Baldwin, an unusually astute ob-
server of twentieth-century American life, "does not
refer merely, or even principally, to the past. On the
contrary, the great force of history comes from the fact that we
carry it within us, are unconsciously controlled by it in many
ways, and history is literally *present* in all that we do."

Rarely has Baldwin's insight been more forcefully con-
firmed than during the past decade. To the surprise of historians themselves, in the final years of the twentieth century and
opening moments of the twenty-first, history seemed to enter
into Americans' public and private consciousness more powerfully than at any time in recent memory. Our equivalent of
what the British call the "heritage industry" reached unprecedented levels of popularity and profitability. Works focused on
history regularly appeared on both fiction and nonfiction best-
seller lists. Hollywood, for better or worse, churned out any
number of historically oriented films, including *Amistad, Gladiator, The Patriot,* and *Pearl Harbor*. There was a spate of efforts to

designate historic buildings like New York's Grand Central Terminal as landmarks, saving them from demolition, and to restore their architectural beauty. The History Channel emerged as one of the most successful enterprises on cable television. Attendance at historical museums and other venues for the public presentation of the past reached new heights. Corporations moved to cash in on Americans' fascination with history. Primedia, the magazine, video, and Internet conglomerate, began sponsoring reenactments of Civil War battles. "First and foremost we're trying to extend our brand into the Civil War category," a company spokesman told a reporter for *The Washington Post*.

This expanding popular fascination with the past coincided, sometimes uneasily, with a profound reorientation of historical scholarship. It has become almost a truism that the past thirty years have witnessed a remarkable expansion of the cast of characters included in historical narratives and the methods employed in historical analysis. Groups neglected by earlier scholars—African-Americans, women, working people, and others—have moved to center stage in accounts of the past, and the professoriat itself has changed so that it more fully reflects the composition of American society. In eight years of undergraduate and graduate study at Columbia University during the 1960s, I never once was taught by a woman or non-white historian. Such an experience would be virtually impossible today.

The new scholarship began to produce a long-overdue diversification of public history. The Freedom Trail, a walking tour of monuments, buildings, and historical markers that has long been Boston's premier tourist attraction, has now been supplemented by a Women's History Trail, a Black Heritage

Trail, and a guide to the city's gay and lesbian history. Civil rights tourism is a growing business in the South. North Carolina officials urge Americans to visit Greensboro, where the sit-ins began in 1960, to see where "four brave people refused to move" and thereby "moved an entire nation." The new Trail of Tears National Historic Trail (commemorating the forced removal of the Cherokee nation from their homes in the 1830s) has been warmly embraced by tourism-conscious town fathers in out-of-the-way places from Georgia to Oklahoma.

On the other hand, the rise of what used to be called the "new social history" has also produced expressions of concern about a fragmentation of scholarship and the difficulty of constructing coherent narratives of the past when historians focus on various groups' distinctive experiences. Practitioners of more traditional fields such as diplomatic, political, and business history have complained repeatedly of feeling marginalized in a profession where social and cultural studies are in the ascendancy. More interesting, in a way, is the gap between the thrust of contemporary scholarship and the hold that "conventional" subjects retain on the broad public interested in history. History best-sellers today deal with topics that would have been familiar decades ago: the founding fathers, the Lewis and Clark expedition, the Civil War, World War II. The History Channel devotes infinitely more time to military history than to runaway slaves or fighters for women's suffrage. The two most popular exhibitions at the National Museum of American History in Washington are those on the presidency and first ladies.

There is nothing unusual or sinister in the fact that each generation rewrites history to suit its own needs, or about disagreements within the profession and among the public at large about how history should best be taught and studied. What was different in the 1990s was history's sudden emergence as a "wedge issue" in the so-called culture wars. During that decade, it sometimes seemed, one could scarcely open a newspaper without encountering bitter controversy over the teaching and presentation of the American past. One series of acrimonious disputes centered on whether the "new history" was producing an insufficiently uplifting version of the nation's development. The Columbus quincentennial of 1992 was all but ruined by debates over whether the anniversary of his "discovery" should be recalled as a source of national pride (the birth of a New World) or shame (the decimation of native populations and introduction of slavery). A planned exhibit at the Smithsonian Institution to mark the fiftieth anniversary of the dropping of the first atomic bomb was denounced by veterans' groups for alleged pro-Japanese bias and for suggesting that the use of the weapon may not have been necessary. In the end, the museum was forced to remove virtually all historical material that was to have accompanied the display of the *Enola Gay*, the plane that bombed Hiroshima. Proposed national standards for the teaching of history were denounced by critics like Lynne Cheney, former head of the National Endowment for the Humanities, for devoting too much attention to obscure members of minority groups, slighting more prominent American leaders, and offering a "depressing" account of the nation's development. These debates achieved a remarkable level of vituperation and oversimplification. One letter to the editor likened the National History Standards to distortions of the past "developed in the councils of the Bolshevik and Nazi parties."

A second set of debates centered on the legacy of slavery and the Civil War. In an essay on historical consciousness, Friedrich Nietzsche spoke of "creative forgetfulness"—how the memory of some aspects of the past is predicated on amnesia about others. Slavery is a case in point. Nowhere is the gap between scholarly inquiry and public perceptions of history more stark. It is probably safe to say that the finest body of American historical writing to appear during the past thirty years has been produced by scholars of slavery and emancipation. This literature has not only established beyond question the centrality of slavery to the history of the United States but has refashioned our understanding of subjects ranging from colonial settlement to the American Revolution and the origins and consequences of the Civil War.

In public history, however, a large void still exists when it comes to slavery. To be sure, communities throughout the North have taken steps to identify and commemorate sites associated with the Underground Railroad, and a museum devoted to slavery and emancipation is being planned for Cincinnati. Visitors to the nation's capital, however, will find a national museum devoted to the Holocaust, funded annually with millions of taxpayer dollars, but almost nothing related to slavery. Tours of historic plantations in the South still largely sugarcoat the slave experience. Of the hundreds of Civil War monuments North and South, only a handful depict the 200,000 African-Americans who fought for the Union. Liverpool and Nantes, two European ports whose wealth derived from the slave trade, have hosted museum exhibits candidly depicting the role of slavery in their growth. No such exhibition has ever been mounted in New York City, which grew rich in the early nineteenth century marketing the products of slave labor.

Nonetheless, slavery has played a prominent role in recent disputes about history. The public display of the Confederate battle flag in the South inspired demonstrations, economic boycotts, and one statewide referendum. The movement for reparations for slavery gained increasing support among black politicians and intellectuals. Pro-Confederate statements by Gale Norton and John Ashcroft, members of George W. Bush's cabinet, spurred public controversy, as did a decision by the New Orleans school board to rechristen public schools that were named for slaveholders, including Confederate generals and some of the nation's founders.

Buffeted by conflicting tides of public sentiment, politicians leaped into the fray, with varied results. President Bill Clinton more or less "apologized" for slavery while on a visit to Africa. The New York state legislature mandated that school history curricula include slavery, the Holocaust, and the Irish famine (and New Jersey added the Armenian genocide)—as if historical identity were defined by separate and equal victimizations. More productively, Congress directed the National Park Service to devote increased attention to slavery at its Civil War sites—recognition that popular venues like Gettysburg presently offer no account of why men actually went to war.

Nietzsche distinguished three approaches to history: the monumental, the antiquarian, and the critical (the first two being history that is celebratory and nostalgic, the third history "that judges and condemns"). Among other things, the 1990s debates revealed that the desire for a history of celebration is widespread and knows no political boundaries. It thrives among minorities hoping to foster a sense of group pride and patriots seeking to encourage love of country. Of course, there is nothing intrinsically wrong with young people either developing from history a sense of identity or taking pride in their nation's accomplishments. But when history locates supposedly primordial characteristics shared with members of one's own group and no one else, it negates the interpenetration of cultures that is so much a part of our nation's past. And when it seeks to return to an earlier narrative emphasizing the glories of American development, it ignores the fact that thanks to the broadened canvas of the "new" histories, it is no longer possible to treat American history as an unalloyed saga of national progress toward liberty and equality.

In every country, versions of the past provide the raw material for nationalist ideologies and patriotic sentiments. The scholarly writing of history—in Europe, where it originated, and in newly independent nations of Asia and Africa in the past generations—has always been tied to the nation-state. In the United States, calls for a more patriotic history have mounted at times of nation building (such as the first half of the nineteenth century), perceived national fragmentation (such as the 1890s or 1990s, decades of widespread concern over mass immigration), and wars. American historians, like their counterparts elsewhere, have often sought to construct an intellectually plausible lineage for the nation, while, until recently, excluding those, such as Indian tribes, African-Americans, or the Spanish- and French-derived cultures of the Mississippi Valley and the trans-Mississippi West, who seemed little more than obstacles to the expansion of Anglo-Saxon liberty and national greatness. The problem with these histories was not simply that they were incomplete, but that they left students utterly unprepared to confront American reality. The civil rights revolution, divisions over Vietnam, Watergate—these seemed to spring from nowhere, without discernible roots in the American past.

Of course, there is nothing distinctively American about controversy over how history should be conceptualized. In recent years, countries around the globe have been roiled by debates over history similar in many ways to our own. Critics condemned a proposed new history curriculum for British schools for not being "British enough"—meaning that it neglected a number of monarchs while requiring students to study non-European societies such as Aztec Mexico or Benin. New official textbooks in Mexico stirred complaints that, in keeping with current government policies, the regime of Porfirio Díaz was praised for promoting economic modernization while the dictatorial aspects of his rule were slighted. In Japan, demonstrators protested the introduction of new texts said to sanitize the country's aggression in World War II and its maltreatment of occupied peoples such as the Koreans and Chinese. In Israel, new scholarship and a public television series that challenged reigning orthodoxies about the nation's founding (for example, that most Arabs who fled the country in the wake of the 1948 war left voluntarily) stirred enormous controversy.

Although they generated far more heat than light, the history wars did underscore the basic differences between historians' understanding of their task and what much of the broader public thinks the writing of history entails. Historians view the constant search for new perspectives as the lifeblood of historical understanding. Outside the academy, however, the act of reinterpretation is often viewed with suspicion, and "revisionist" is invoked as a term of abuse. At a Senate hearing on the Smithsonian controversy, Senator Dianne Feinstein of California remarked that when she studied history as a Stanford undergraduate, her professors confined themselves to presenting facts. Now, she complained, historians are engaged in interpretation. Surely her Stanford classes must have introduced Senator Feinstein to the writings of giants of scholarship like

Carl Becker and Charles Beard, who nearly a century ago demolished the notion that historical truth is fixed and permanent and that fact and interpretation can be sealed off from each other. The very selection and ordering of some "facts" while ignoring others is itself an act of interpretation. I am reminded of my conversation during the history standards debate with an eager young reporter from *Newsweek*. "Professor," she asked, "when did historians stop relating facts and start all this revising of interpretations of the past?" Around the time of Thucydides, I told her.

History always has been and always will be regularly rewritten, in response to new questions, new information, new methodologies, and new political, social, and cultural imperatives. But that each generation can and must rewrite history does not mean that history is simply a series of myths and inventions. There are commonly accepted professional standards that enable us to distinguish good history from falsehoods like the denial of the Holocaust. Historical truth does exits, not in the scientific sense but as a reasonable approximation of the past. But the most difficult truth for those outside the ranks of professional historians to accept is that there often exists more than one legitimate way of recounting past events.

Thankfully, the history wars appear to have subsided. But these controversies raised a set of questions relating to the politics and purposes of historical understanding central to the essays in this book. As my graduate school mentor Richard Hofstadter once observed, the best rationale for collections such as this may be the simple one of accessibility—bringing together in a single volume pieces originally published in obscure corners of the academic world. But, he added, such a collection also possesses value in illustrating a common cast of mind, for whatever their subject matter, the essays are "unified by some underlying intellectual intent [and] a set of related concerns."

Written between 1983 and 2001, the essays that follow all deal, in one way or another, with the relationship between the historian and his or her own world. The first two look back on my own career and that of Hofstadter himself. They suggest how the context within which a historian lives and writes affects one's choice of subject and approach to the past. The next four essays look at broad international changes of the past two decades—the accelerating pace of globalization, the collapse of the Soviet Union and of the apartheid state in South Africa, and the decline of socialism—to consider their effect on historical consciousness. The final three examine the enduring but often misunderstood legacy of slavery, the Civil War, and Reconstruction for contemporary American society. In these essays, the Reconstruction era that followed the war plays a major role, not only because I have devoted much of my scholarly career to its study but also because it illustrates most forcefully the interconnections of past and present.

Given the partisan exaggerations and intellectual distortions so evident in the historical controversies of the 1990s, it would be perfectly understandable if historians retreated altogether from engagement with the larger public. This, I believe, would be a serious mistake. A century ago, in his presidential address to the American Historical Association, Charles Francis Adams called on historians to step outside the ivory tower and engage forthrightly in public discourse. The study of history, he insisted, had a "public function," and historians had an obligation to contribute to debates in which history was frequently invoked with little genuine understanding or knowledge. "The standard of American political discussion," Adams pointedly remarked, "is not now so high as not to admit of elevation," and invocations of history should not be left to "the journalist and the politician." These observations are as relevant today as in 1900, when Adams spoke.

Who owns history? Everyone and no one—which is why the study of the past is a constantly evolving, never-ending journey of discovery.

PART I

THE POLITICS
OF HISTORY
AND HISTORIANS

ONE

MY LIFE AS A HISTORIAN

In 1996, the department of history at Fordham University invited a group of American historians whose work had focused on the history of race in the United States to speak about the influences that had shaped our choices of career and subject matter.

•

H istorians, by and large, are not noted for introspection. Our calling requires us to analyze past events, but we rarely turn our interpretive talents upon ourselves. I welcome the opportunity to reflect publicly about how and why I became a historian, how my approach to the study of history has changed over time, and how the concerns of the present have helped to shape the questions I ask about the past.

Born in New York City in 1943, I was raised in Long Beach, Long Island, to all outward appearances a typical child of America's postwar suburban boom. In one respect, however, my upbringing was unusual, although emblematic nonetheless of one aspect of the American experience. Shortly before I was born, my father, Jack D. Foner, and uncle, Philip S. Foner, both historians at City College in New York, were among some sixty faculty members dismissed from teaching positions at the City University after informers named them as members of the Communist party at hearings of the state legislature's notorious Rapp-Coudert Committee, a precursor of McCarthyism. A few years later, my mother was forced to resign from her job as a high school art teacher. During my childhood and for many years afterward, my parents were blacklisted and unable to teach. Unlike most of my generation, I did not have to wait until the upheavals of the 1960s to discover the yawning gap that separated America's professed ideals and its self-confident claim to be a land of liberty from its social and political reality. My friend Gabor S. Boritt, who grew up in communist Hungary and now directs the Civil War Institute at Gettysburg College, once remarked to me, "I was raised in a country where we understood that most of what the government says is untrue." "That's funny," I replied, "I grew up in the same country."

Given the profession of my father and uncle, it seems in retrospect inevitable that I would become a historian. But, as I frequently tell my students, events are inevitable only after they happen. As a youth I wanted to be an astronomer, and my first published book was entitled *The Solar System*. To be sure, "published" is a bit of an exaggeration. The book, with one chapter on each planet, was dictated by me, typed by my mother, and illustrated by a family friend. It was not based on archival research. But I was only seven years old at the time.

My greatest joy as a youth was gazing through a telescope on spring nights, and my idea of athletic prowess was serving on the Long Beach High School math team (we finished second in Long Island one year). But I also imbibed a lively interest in both history and current events. Historical and political concerns suffused our household. Every child thinks his upbringing is entirely normal. Only gradually did I realize that other families did not discuss the intricacies of international relations and domestic politics over the dinner table, or follow election returns in France, India, and Guatemala as avidly as those in the United States.

What was truly distinctive about my family's view of both American history and the world around us, however, was our preoccupation with the past and present condition of our black fellow countrymen. As suburbs go, Long Beach was a liberal community, whose predominantly Jewish residents regularly voted Democratic. But on issues relating to race, the prevailing sentiment was indifference. Our idyllic town had its own small ghetto, home to black domestic servants, but no one except my parents and a few like-minded friends seemed aware of its existence, or wondered why housing there was so inferior to that enjoyed by whites. In school, we did commemorate Negro History Week, mostly with lessons about George Washington Carver and his amazing feats with peanuts. But our history texts were typical of the time: slavery, they taught, was a regrettable but not particularly oppressive institution, Reconstruction a terrible mistake, and blacks played no discernible role whatever in the rest of American history. I well recall my mother (to my embarrassment) striding into school to complain about the illustrations of happy slaves playing banjos in our primary school history text. The principal could not understand her unhappiness. "What difference does it make," he asked, "what we teach them about slavery?"

5

In my home, however, it made a great deal of difference. As the work of Mark Naison and other scholars has shown, in the 1930s the Communist party was the only predominantly white organization to make fighting racism central to its political program. Communist-oriented historians like Herbert Aptheker and my uncle Philip Foner, along with black scholars like W.E.B. Du Bois, had begun the process of challenging prevailing stereotypes about black history. At home, I learned ideas that today are taken for granted but then were virtually unknown outside black and left-wing circles: slavery was the fundamental cause of the Civil War and emancipation its greatest accomplishment; Reconstruction was a tragedy not because it was attempted but because it failed; and the condition of blacks was the nation's foremost domestic problem. Du Bois and Paul Robeson were friends of my family, Frederick Douglass (whom my uncle had rescued from historical oblivion by publishing a four-volume collection of his magnificent writings and speeches) a household name. In my home, we followed with a growing sense of excitement the unfolding of the civil rights movement, and it was assumed that my younger brother and I would participate in it. Tom went on to take part in the Mississippi Freedom Summer of 1964. I attended not only the March on Washington of 1963 but also the less well-known march of 1957, and in 1960 I spent a great deal of time picketing Woolworth stores in New York in support of the Southern sit-ins. By then, I was a freshman at Columbia College, where during my undergraduate years I became the first president of ACTION, a student political party that, along with sponsoring folk music concerts, issued newsletters on civil rights and persuaded the off-campus housing registry to drop listings from landlords who would not sign a nondiscrimination pledge.

I entered Columbia fully intending to major in astronomy. By the end of my sophomore year, my interest—or perhaps my talent—in science had waned considerably. Then, in my junior year, I somehow persuaded James P. Shenton to allow me to enroll in his senior seminar on the Civil War period. By the end of the year, I was not only a history major but had developed what has become a lifelong passion for that era.

Looking back over my career, I realize that I learned from two great teachers what it is to be a historian. The first was my father. Deprived of his livelihood while I was growing up, he supported our family as a freelance lecturer on history and current affairs. Listening to his lectures, I came to appreciate how present concerns can be illuminated by the study of the past—how the repression of the McCarthy era recalled the days of the Alien and Sedition Acts, how the civil rights movement needed to be viewed in light of the great struggles of black and white abolitionists, and how in the brutal suppression of the Philippine insurrection at the turn of the century could be found the antecedents of American intervention in Iran, Guatemala, and Vietnam. I also imbibed a way of thinking about the past in which visionaries and underdogs—Tom Paine, Wendell Phillips, Eugene.V. Debs, and W.E.B. Du Bois— were as central to the historical drama as presidents and captains of industry, and how a commitment to social justice could infuse one's attitudes toward the past. The second great teacher was Jim Shenton, legendary at Columbia for his dramatic lecturing style and the personal interest he took in his students— down to introducing us to the city's culinary attractions. From Shenton, I learned that successful teaching rests both on a genuine and selfless concern for students and on the ability to convey to them a love of history.

My seminar paper that year was a study of the Free Soil party of 1848, a justifiably obscure topic that led to my first excursion into archival research, in my senior thesis, supervised by Richard Hofstadter. The fact that the civil rights movement was then reaching its crescendo powerfully affected my choice of subject: the racial attitudes of those who opposed the expansion of slavery. Just two years earlier, Leon Litwack had stunned the historical profession with his demonstration, in *North of Slavery*, that racism was every bit as pervasive in the antebellum North as in the slave South. My research built on his insight, to demonstrate that many Free Soilers opposed the expansion of slavery in order to keep blacks, free or slave, from competing with "free white labor."

My senior thesis became the basis of my first two published articles, which appeared in 1965. More importantly, it introduced me to Hofstadter, the premier historian of his generation, who would soon be supervising my dissertation. One day Hofstadter related to me how he had obtained his first full-time teaching position when a job opened in 1941 at the downtown branch of City College because of the dismissal of a victim of the Rapp-Coudert Committee. Students initially boycotted Hofstadter's lectures as a show of support for his purged predecessor, but eventually they returned to the classroom. Ironically, Hofstadter's first job resulted from the flourishing of the kind of political paranoia that he would later lament in his historical writings. Even more ironically, the victim of political blacklisting whom Hofstadter replaced was my father.

Whatever thoughts he harbored about this twist of fate, Hofstadter played brilliantly the role of intellectual mentor so crucial to any student's career. His books directed me toward the subjects that have defined much of my own writing—the history of political ideologies and the interconnections between social development and political culture. Years later I learned that it was thanks to Hofstadter that on graduating from college, I was awarded a Kellett Fellowship to study at Oriel College, Oxford. The tutorial system, in which the student prepares a paper each week and reads it aloud to the tutor, gave me invaluable training in quick, clear expository writing. Each week I was forced to master a subject about which I previously knew nothing—the reasons for the decline of the medieval wool trade, for example—and to present my ideas in a coherent fashion. I probably owe it to my years at Oxford that writer's block has never been one of my problems. At the end of my stay, I decided to return to Columbia to pursue a doctorate in American history. My decision was not greeted with universal enthusiasm. When I told my tutor, W. A. Pantin, a specialist on the English church in the fourteenth century, that I wanted to devote my career to the American past, he replied: "In other words, you have ceased to study history."

I returned to Columbia in 1965. While I was away, the sixties had happened. Students now wore long hair and colorful attire and spent much of their time imbibing substances of questionable legality. Vietnam had replaced race as the predominant issue on campus; it would soon become the catalyst for a full-fledged generational rebellion. Like so many others, I threw myself into the antiwar movement, but intellectually I remained preoccupied with issues surrounding slavery and race, a preoccupation that deepened as America's cities burned between 1965 and 1968, the civil rights movement evaporated, and it became clear that racism was far more deeply entrenched in American life than we had imagined a few short years before.

Somehow, while participating in events from antiwar marches to the Columbia student rebellion of 1968, I managed to write my dissertation, which became the basis of my first book, *Free Soil, Free Labor, Free Men.* A study of the ideology of the Republican party before the Civil War, the dissertation grew out of my old interest in free soilism. Among my aims was to outline Republicans' complex attitudes toward blacks, but I was deeply impressed by a comment by Winthrop Jordan at a conference I attended in 1966: "To understand people's attitudes about race, you have to understand their attitudes about everything." Jordan's remark helped me conceptualize my theme as a study of ideology—the coherent worldview that brought together reinforcing attitudes about labor, economic growth, westward expansion, and race relations, and which inspired Republicans to oppose slavery's expansion and the growth of Southern political power. Published in 1970, my book became part of a trend whereby American historians rediscovered the value of the concept of ideology. Events of the time strongly influenced this development. In a society engulfed by social crisis, it no longer seemed plausible to argue, with 1950s "consensus" historians, that Americans had never disagreed profoundly over social and political issues.

To one looking back from the vantage point of thirty years, *Free Soil* seems a curiously old-fashioned book. Written, as it were, on the threshold separating two generations of historical scholarship, it lacked the benefit of the "new histories" that have matured since its publication in 1970 and that have focused historians' attention on the experiences of ordinary men and women rather than political leaders. History education at Columbia in those days resolutely favored the political and intellectual. But when I returned to England for the

1972–73 academic year to pursue work for my next project, a history of American radicalism, I encountered the new social and labor history. My historical writing would never be the same. Today, when we take for granted that history must include the experience of previously neglected groups—blacks, women, laborers, and others—it is difficult to recapture the sense of intellectual excitement produced by the works of E. P. Thompson, Eric Hobsbawm, and other British practitioners of "history from below." Thanks to what came to be called the "new social history," which they inspired, we today have a far more complex and nuanced portrait of the American past, in all its diversity and contentiousness.

Of course, the inclusion of these diverse experiences in teaching and writing is not without its difficulties, as I had already discovered. In 1969, I was offered a job as an instructor in history at Columbia. As the department's junior member, I soon found myself representing history on doctoral dissertations from other departments, with fascinating subjects like "Tree Imagery in Emerson" and "The Belgian Press and the Boer War." But the main reason I was hired was to teach Columbia's first course in African-American history. My qualifications lay in a course on the subject that I had offered in Double Discovery, a summer program for minority high school students, and my writings on free soil and race. Inevitably and understandably, many of Columbia's black students felt that the first such course in the College's two-hundred-year history ought to be offered by a black scholar. But I was eager to teach the course and insisted—as I continue to believe—that teaching and writing in black history should be held to the same standards as in any other academic discipline. The race of the instructor is not among them.

At any rate, I prepared avidly for the course, reading everything I could get my hands on, and for the first few weeks my expertise disarmed my critics. But a month into the term, a group of black students began demonstrating both in and out of class, denouncing the course, in the idiom of the day, as a racist insult. For the rest of the term, there were walkouts and disruptions. Yet most of the 150 students in the class attended every lecture and seemed eager to hear me teach the subject. (As they told me privately, they actually liked my lectures and had nothing "personal" against me.) After this baptism by fire, nothing that has happened in a classroom has ever fazed me. Out of that course came my next two publications: *America's Black Past*, an anthology of writings in the field, and *Nat Turner*, a documentary collection about America's greatest slave rebel. Since 1969, I have taught black history many times with little problem. Equally importantly, over the years I have fully integrated the black experience into my general courses on nineteenth-century history.

My initial career at Columbia lasted only three years. While I was in England, the department informed me that I should not expect to receive tenure. I was bitterly disappointed, but this rebuff turned out to be an immense stroke of good fortune. City College had just hired Herbert Gutman to revitalize its history department, and Herb offered me a job. So in 1973, I moved to a college that was one mile uptown from Columbia but was as remote from it in other ways as if it were located on the far side of the moon. City was in the throes of adjusting to open admissions, with a faculty bitterly divided against itself. At my first department meeting, one colleague called another "a perjured slanderer," whereupon the second launched a lawsuit for defamation of character. But coming to City was the best thing that had ever happened to me, both as a teacher and a historian. It brought me into contact with an entirely different group of students—the children of the city's white ethnic, black, and Hispanic working class, nearly all of them the first members of their families to attend college. Some were woefully unprepared, while others were quite ready to take advantage of the opportunity that had suddenly been opened to them. Life at City was by turns inspiring and frustrating, but I have no doubt that the challenge made me a much better teacher.

Equally remarkable was the intellectual community Gutman had assembled, including brilliant young American historians like Leon Fink, Virginia Yans, and Eric Perkins. At the center of the group stood Gutman himself, with his irrepressible enthusiasm for recovering the history of forgotten Americans, from coal miners and silk workers in Gilded Age America to slaves. Under his influence, my education as a historian continued apace. My next book, *Tom Paine and Revolutionary America*, was powerfully influenced both by my recent stay in England and by Gutman's work. Like *Free Soil*, this was essentially a study of political ideology, but now I grounded Paine's writings firmly in the social history of his diverse environments, especially lower-class London and Philadelphia, and explored the role of social movements, not just political parties, in the dissemination of political ideas.

Having completed *Tom Paine*, I prepared to return to my long-delayed history of American radicalism. (Paine was supposed to have been the first chapter, but when I sat down to write it, the chapter had come to more than two hundred pages, a book in its own right.) But fate, in the person of Richard Morris, intervened. Totally unexpectedly, Morris invited me to write the volume on Reconstruction for the New American Nation series, of which he and Henry Steele Commager were editors. Although I had written nothing on Reconstruction except for an essay on Thaddeus Stevens (another prospective chapter in my ill-fated radicalism book), I had long had an interest in this, the most controversial and misunderstood period in all of American history.

Years before, I had presented my own interpretation of Reconstruction to my ninth-grade American history class at Long Beach High School. Our teacher was Mrs. Bertha Berryman, affectionately known among the students as Big Bertha (after a famous piece of World War I artillery). Following the then-dominant view of the era, Mrs. Berryman described the Reconstruction Act of 1867, which gave the right to vote to black men in the South, as the worst law in all of American history. I raised my hand and proposed that the Alien and Sedition Acts were "worse." Whereupon Mrs. Berryman replied, "If you don't like the way I'm teaching, Eric, why don't you come in tomorrow and give your own lesson on Reconstruction?" This I proceeded to do, admittedly with my father's help, in a presentation based largely on W.E.B. Du Bois's portrait of Reconstruction as a pivotal moment in the struggle for democracy in America. At the end of the class, Mrs. Berryman, herself a true democrat, announced: "Class, you have heard me, and you have heard Eric. Now let us vote to see who was right." I wish I could report that my persuasive presentation carried the day. In fact, only one student voted for me, my intrepid friend Neil Kleinman.

It therefore seemed almost preordained when Morris offered me the chance to get even with Mrs. Berryman. I soon discovered that I had agreed to take on a project with a checkered past. In 1948, Howard K. Beale had agreed to do the book; he died eleven years later without having written a word. He was succeeded by David Donald. In 1969, Donald published an article lamenting that he had found it impossible to synthesize in a single account the political, economic, social, and intellectual developments of the era, and the course of national, Northern, and Southern events. The effort to do so seemed to make him despair of the entire enterprise of chronicling the nation's past. He had come to the conclusion, Donald wrote, that "the United States does not have a history." In 1975, he abandoned the project to devote himself to a more manageable one, a biography of Thomas Wolfe.

Fools, they say, rush in where angels fear to tread. I assumed I could do a year or two of reading and complete the book soon afterward. In fact, it took about ten years to research and write it. The turning point in my conceptualization of the project came in 1978, when I was invited to teach for a semester at the University of South Carolina in Columbia. There, in the state archives, I encountered 121 thickly packed boxes of correspondence received by the state's Reconstruction governors. The letters contained an incredibly rich record, almost entirely untapped by scholars, of local social and political life in the state. Before my eyes unfolded tales of utopian hopes and shattered dreams, of struggles for human dignity and ignoble violence by the Ku Klux Klan, of racism and black-white cooperation, of how everyday life had become "politicized" in ways barely hinted at in the existing literature. I realized that to tell the story of Reconstruction, I could not rely on available scholarship, impressive as much of it was, but would have to delve into the archives to recover the local texture of life. In ensuing years, my research introduced me to an amazing cast of characters—former slaves seeking to breathe substantive meaning into the freedom they had acquired, upcountry farmers struggling to throw off the heritage of racism, planters seeking to retain control of their now-emancipated labor force, and Klansmen seeking to subvert the far-reaching changes of the era. Like Du Bois half a century earlier, I became convinced that the freed people were the central actors in the drama of Reconstruction. Rather than simply victims of manipulation or passive recipients of the actions of others, they were agents of change, whose demand for individual and community autonomy helped to establish the agenda of Reconstruction politics.

Another unexpected development also affected the project's conceptualization. For the 1980–81 academic year, I was invited to teach as the Pitt Professor of American History at Cambridge University. Once again a stay in England broadened my horizons as a historian. Prompted by some of my colleagues, I began to read about the aftermath of slavery in the British Empire, especially in the Caribbean and South Africa. I soon discovered that this literature, much of it unknown to scholars of American history, approached the transition from slavery to freedom in rather different ways from our own historical writing. Instead of defining the problem primarily as one of race relations, the predominant view in this country, scholars in Britain, Africa, and the Caribbean focused attention on the labor question after slavery—how former slaves struggled to secure economic autonomy while former planters, often aided by the British government, sought to encourage them to return to work on the plantations and, when unsuccessful, imported indentured laborers from China and India to take their place. The same issues of access to economic resources and control of labor, I became convinced, were central to the aftermath of slavery in the Reconstruction South. But my reading also underscored for me the uniqueness of Reconstruction, for only in this country were former slaves, within a few years of emancipation, given the right to vote, and only here did they exercise a significant degree of political power on the state and local levels. Historians at that time were prone to describe Reconstruction as essentially conservative, since it adhered to constitutional forms and did not distribute land to the former slaves. I became convinced that enfranchising the freedmen constituted, both in a comparative perspective and in the context of the racism of antebellum America, a truly radical experiment in interracial democracy.

In 1982, I returned to Columbia to teach, and here over the next few years the book was written. There is a certain irony in the fact that a Columbia historian produced this new history of Reconstruction, exemplified by the fact that my research expenses were partly covered by the department's Dunning Fund and much of my reading took place in Burgess Library. For it was at Columbia at the turn of the century that William A. Dunning and John W. Burgess had established the traditional school of Reconstruction scholarship, teaching that blacks were "children" incapable of appreciating the freedom that had been thrust upon them, and that the North did a "monstrous thing" in granting them suffrage. There is no better illustration than Reconstruction of how historical interpretation both reflects and helps to shape current policies. The views of the Dunning School helped freeze the white South for generations in unalterable opposition to any change in race relations, and justified decades of Northern indifference to Southern nullification of the Fourteenth and Fifteenth Amendments. The civil rights revolution, in turn, produced an outpouring of revisionist literature, far more favorable to the aspirations of the former slaves.

I think it was the historian C. Vann Woodward who first called the civil rights movement the Second Reconstruction. Although history never really repeats itself, the parallels between the period after the Civil War and the 1950s and 1960s are very dramatic, as are the retreats from the Reconstruction ideal of racial justice and social equality in the latter decades of the nineteenth century and again in our own time. The issues that agitate race relations today—affirmative action, the role of the federal government in enforcing the rights of citizens, the possibility of interracial political coalitions, the relationship between economic and political equality—were also central to the debates of Reconstruction. Most strikingly, perhaps, both Reconstructions failed adequately to address the economic plight of black America, itself the legacy of 250 years of slavery and a century of segregation. The first Reconstruction did not respond to the former slaves' thirst for land. The second, which gave rise to a large black middle class, left millions of blacks trapped in decaying urban centers and deindustrializing sectors of the economy. Like the Reconstruction generation, we have seen radical movements rise to prominence, then retreat and shatter. Like them, we have seen the resurgence of ideologies of social Darwinism, biological inferiority, and states' rights that blame the victims of discrimination for their plight or insist that the federal government must not interfere with local traditions of inequality. Just as the failure of the first Reconstruction left to future generations an unfinished agenda of racial and social justice, the waning of the second has shown how far America still has to go in living up to the ideal of equality.

Published in 1988, my book on Reconstruction received a gratifying response—it won several prizes from historical organizations, was a finalist for the National Book Award, and sold far more copies than I was accustomed to. Reviewers praised its voluminous research and the way I integrated the era's numerous themes into a coherent whole. But ultimately, the book's merits derive from the fact that I care deeply about the issues of racial justice central to Reconstruction and to our society today. If *Reconstruction* was born in the archives, it was written from the heart.

With the publication of *Reconstruction,* I assumed I would turn my scholarly attention to other areas. But things have not turned out this way. In the course of my research, I had gathered an immense file of biographical information about black political leaders in the postwar South—justices of the peace, sheriffs, and state legislators, as well as congressmen and U.S. senators—most of them unknown even to scholars. I brought this information together in *Freedom's Lawmakers,* a directory containing capsule biographies of some fifteen hundred individuals. Their treatment by past historians strikingly illustrated how racism and a commitment to maintaining white supremacy in the South had warped scholarly writing. Generations of historians had ignored or denigrated these black officeholders, citing their alleged incompetence in order to justify the violent overthrow of Reconstruction and the South's long history of disenfranchising black voters. Claude Bowers's sensationalist best-seller of the 1920s, *The Tragic Era,* described Louisiana's Reconstruction legislature as a "zoo"; E. Merton Coulter wrote in 1947 that black officeholding was "the most exotic development in government in the history of white civilization . . . [and the] longest to be remembered, shuddered at, and execrated." My hope was to put these men, as it were, on the map of history, to make available the basic data concerning their lives, and to bury irrevocably the misconception that Reconstruction's leaders were illiterate, propertyless, and incompetent.

As *Freedom's Lawmakers* indicates, I seem unable to escape the Reconstruction era. I am currently the historical adviser for a television documentary on the period and recently served as curator of a museum exhibition—the first ever to be devoted exclusively to the period—that opened in 1995 at the Virginia Historical Society in Richmond and subsequently traveled to venues in New York City, Columbia, Raleigh, Tallahassee, and Chicago. This last project emerged from another unexpected twist in my career: my emergence as something of a public historian.

Shortly before I finished my book on Reconstruction, I was asked by the Chicago Historical Society to develop—along with one of their curators, Olivia Mahoney—a major exhibition on the Civil War era. My initial response was that they had approached the wrong person. I have no background in the study of material culture or in museum work. As a teacher, I am resolutely old-fashioned—until very recently, I never used slides, films, or the Internet in teaching, except for a tattered map of the United States that I began tacking to the classroom wall after discovering that students in New York City do not know the location of the Mississippi River. But, the society's directors assured me, they had plenty of staff who could design exhibitions. What they needed was up-to-date historical thinking. For years, one of their most popular rooms had been the Lincoln Gallery, a collection of memorabilia such as the Great

Emancipator's top hat, a piece of wood from his log cabin, some photos, and dioramas of scenes, real and mythic, from his life. The exhibition was popular, but it was not history. The society proposed to replace it with a full-scale account of the causes and conduct of the Civil War. As curator, my job was to outline the major historical themes, write labels, and, working with Mahoney, choose the objects to be included in the show. The only stipulation was that the exhibit had to include the bed on which Lincoln died after being shot at Ford's Theater. This had somehow come into the society's possession, and people traveled from far and wide to see it. Otherwise, I had complete intellectual freedom—I could do and say pretty much anything I wanted.

Like other historians, I have often lamented that scholars too often speak only to themselves and seem to have abandoned the effort to address a broader public. How could I refuse this invitation to help shape how hundreds of thousands of visitors who might never have attended a university history class or read an academic treatise understand a pivotal era of our country's history? So I accepted, thus embarking on what became, for me, a thoroughly enjoyable process of learning by doing. The finished exhibit, *A House Divided: America in the Age of Lincoln*, is unabashedly interpretive. It explores the contrast between free and slave labor and the societies built upon them, focuses on slavery as the primary cause of the Civil War, devotes attention both to abolitionism and to Northern racism, and as it gives an account of the military history of the war, also stresses the process of emancipation as central to the war's meaning. Lincoln is present, but as a figure located firmly within his own time, not an icon standing outside it. The exhibit has been a great success, not only winning several awards but inspiring other museums to bring in historians to upgrade outdated presentations of history.

My new role in public history involved me in a realm that was suddenly filled with controversy—witness the evisceration in the mid-1990s of the Smithsonian Institution's proposed exhibition on the dropping of the first atomic bomb, or the Library of Congress canceling a small show on the life and material surroundings of slaves. Of course, vigorous debate about how history should be studied and taught is healthy and inevitable in a democratic society. But too often critics of innovative exhibitions—whether veterans' groups in the case of the Smithsonian, or black employees of the Library of Congress— reveal a desire for a history that eliminates complexity from our national experience. The overwhelmingly positive reactions to the two historical exhibitions on which I worked suggest that visitors actually enjoy encountering new ideas and having their preconceptions challenged by unfamiliar interpretations. The public seems to be more open-minded, more willing to learn, than those who desire a purely celebratory public history are prepared to believe.

Only recently have my scholarly interests moved on from Reconstruction. My latest book, *The Story of American Freedom*, published in 1998, traces how various Americans have interpreted and defined freedom, so central an element of our national consciousness, from the Revolution to the present. The book builds on my earlier writings on free labor, emancipation, and Reconstruction, but unlike my previous work, it brings me into the twentieth century. My theme is that rather than a fixed category or predetermined concept, freedom has always been a terrain of struggle. Its definition has been constantly created and re-created, its meanings constructed not only in congressional debates and political treatises but on plantations and picket lines, in parlors and bedrooms. It has been invoked by those in power to legitimate their aims, and seized upon by others seeking to transform society. In our own time, we have seen the putative division of the planet into free and nonfree worlds invoked by our government to justify violations of individual liberties at home and support for some highly repressive governments abroad. Yet within my lifetime as well, the greatest mass movement of the century reinvigorated the language of freedom with its freedom rides, freedom songs, and the insistent cry "Freedom now!" The story of American freedom, in other words, is as contentious, as multidimensional, as American society itself.

Let me close, however, by looking back to the mid-1990s, when I again spent the academic year in England, this time as Harmsworth Professor of American History at Oxford. Once again, living there seemed to expand my intellectual horizons, bringing me into contact, just as I was embarking on my study of freedom, with social historians of language and historians of political thought. But the year's highlight came not in England but five thousand miles to the south. In the summer of 1994, I was invited to lecture in South Africa, shortly after it had experienced its first democratic elections. To me as a historian of Reconstruction, the photographs, broadcast around the world, of men and women waiting on endless lines to cast their first ballots brought to mind the scenes of celebration in our own country when former slaves voted for the first time after the Civil War. It was a reminder, in these days of cynicism about politics and democracy, that voting can be a deeply empowering act.

On the day before I left South Africa, I delivered the
T. B. Davie Memorial Lecture at the University of Cape Town,
named in honor of a vice-chancellor who courageously defended academic freedom during the 1950s. Thirty-five years
earlier, when the government imposed apartheid on South
African universities, students had marched to the Parliament to
extinguish a torch of freedom. After my lecture, the torch was
relit to symbolize the birth of a new South Africa. It was a
moment of genuine emotion, illustrating the interconnected-
ness of past, present, and future. It seemed to me fitting that a
historian was chosen to speak at this occasion, and it was an
honor for me to be the one, especially since I know from my
own family's experience how fragile freedom can be.

TWO

THE EDUCATION OF
RICHARD HOFSTADTER

In 1992, Beacon Press invited me to write the introduction to a new printing of *Social Darwinism in American Thought,* the book that launched Richard Hofstadter's career as a historian. The essay allowed me to reflect on how Hofstadter's times affected his brilliant historical scholarship.

•

Two decades have now elapsed since the untimely death of Richard Hofstadter. Despite the sweeping transformation of historical scholarship during these years, his writings continue to exert a powerful influence on how scholars and general readers alike understand the American past. Since his death in 1970, the study of political ideas—the recurring theme of Hofstadter's work—has to a considerable extent been eclipsed by histories of family life, race relations, popular culture, and a host of other social concerns. The writings of many of his contemporaries are now all but forgotten. Yet because of his penetrating intellect and sparkling literary style, Hofstadter still commands the attention of anyone who wishes to think seriously about the American past. The reissue of his first book, *Social Darwinism in American Thought*, provides an opportune moment to consider the circumstances of its composition and the reasons for its enduring influence.

Richard Hofstadter was born in 1916 in Buffalo, New York, the son of a Jewish father and a mother of German Lutheran descent. After graduating from high school in 1933, he entered the University of Buffalo, where he majored in philosophy and minored in history. As for so many others of his generation, Hofstadter's formative intellectual and political experience was the Great Depression. Buffalo, a major industrial center, was particularly hard hit by unemployment and social dislocation. The Depression, he later recalled, "started me thinking about the world. . . . It was as clear as day that something had to change. . . . You had to decide, in the first instance, whether you were a Marxist or an American liberal."[1] At the university, Hofstadter gravitated toward a group of left-wing students, including the brilliant and "sometimes overpowering" (as Alfred Kazin later described her) Felice Swados, read Marx and Lenin, and joined the Young Communist League.[2]

In 1936, on the eve of his graduation, Hofstadter and Felice were married and subsequently moved to New York City. Felice first worked for the National Maritime Union and the International Ladies' Garment Workers Union and then took a job as a copy editor at *Time*, while Hofstadter enrolled in the graduate history program at Columbia University. Both became part of New York's broad radical political culture that centered on the Communist party in the era of the Popular Front. Hofstadter would later describe himself (with some exaggeration) as "by temperament quite conservative and timid and acquiescent,"[3] and it seems that the dynamic Felice, a committed political activist, animated their engagement with radicalism. Nonetheless, politics for Hofstadter was much more than a passing fancy; he identified himself as a Marxist and, in apartment discussions and in his correspondence with Felice's brother Harvey Swados, took part in the doctrinal debates between Communists, Trotskyists, Schachtmanites, and others who flourished in the world of New York's radical intelligentsia.

In 1938, Hofstadter joined the Communist party's unit at Columbia. The decision, taken with some reluctance (he had already startled some of his friends by concluding that the Moscow purge trials were "phony"), reflected a craving for decisive action after "the hours I have spent jawing about the thing." As he explained to his brother-in-law: "I join without enthusiasm but with a sense of obligation. . . . My fundamental reason for joining is that I don't like capitalism and want to get rid of it. I am tired of talking. . . . The party is making a very profound contribution to the radicalization of the American people. . . . I prefer to go along with it now."[4]

Hofstadter, however, did not prove to be a very committed party member. He found meetings "dull" and chafed at what he considered the party's intellectual regimentation. By February 1939, he had "quietly eased myself out." His break became irreversible in September, after the announcement of the Nazi-Soviet Pact.[5] There followed a rapid and deep disillusionment—with the party (run by "glorified clerks"), with the Soviet Union ("essentially undemocratic"), and eventually with Marxism itself.[6] Yet for some years, Hofstadter continued to regard himself as a radical. "I hate capitalism and everything that goes with it," he wrote Harvey Swados soon after leaving the party.

Never again, however, would he devote his energies in any sustained manner to a political cause. He became more and more preoccupied with the thought that intellectuals were unlikely to find a comfortable home in any socialist society that was likely to emerge in his lifetime. "People like us . . . ," he wrote, "have become permanently alienated from the spirit of revolutionary movements. . . . We are not the beneficiaries of capitalism, but we will not be the beneficiaries of the socialism of the 20th century. We are the people with no place to go."[7]

Although Hofstadter abandoned active politics after 1939, his earliest work as a historian reflected his continuing intellectual engagement with radicalism. His Columbia master's thesis, written in 1938, dealt with the plight of Southern sharecroppers, a contemporary problem that had become the focus of intense organizing efforts by socialists and communists.[8] Hofstadter showed how the benefits of New Deal agricultural policies in the cotton states flowed to large landowners, while the sharecroppers' conditions only worsened. The essay presented a devastating indictment of the Roosevelt administration for pandering to the South's undemocratic elite. Its critical evaluation of Roosevelt, a common attitude among New York radicals, would persist in Hofstadter's writings long after the political impulse that inspired the thesis had faded.

As with many others who came of age in the 1930s, Hofstadter's general intellectual approach was framed by Marxism, but in application to the American past, the iconoclastic materialism of Charles A. Beard was his greatest inspiration. "Beard was really *the* exciting influence on me," Hofstadter later remarked.[9] Beard taught that American history had been shaped by the struggle of competing economic groups, primarily farmers, industrialists, and workers. Underlying the clashing rhetoric of political leaders lay naked self-interest; the Civil War, for example, should be understood essentially as a transfer of political power from Southern agrarians to Northern capitalists. Differences over the tariff had more to do with its origins than the debate over slavery. Hofstadter's first published essay, a "note" in a 1938 issue of the *American Historical Review*, took issue with Beard's emphasis on the tariff as a basic cause of the Civil War, while accepting the premise that economic self-interest lay at the root of political behavior.[10] (The homestead issue, Hofstadter argued, far outweighed the tariff as a source of sectional tension.) The article inaugurated a dialogue with the Beardian tradition that shaped much of Hofstadter's subsequent career.

While Beard devoted little attention to political ideas, seeing them as mere masks for economic self-interest, Hofstadter soon became attracted to the study of American social thought. His interest was encouraged by Merle Curti, a Marxist Columbia professor with whom Hofstadter by 1939 had formed, according to Felice, a "mutual admiration society."[11] Other than his relationship with Curti, however, Hofstadter was not particularly happy at Columbia. For three years running, he was refused financial aid. Hofstadter was gripped by a sense of unfair treatment. "The guys who got the fellowships," he complained, "are little shits who never accomplished or published anything."[12] (None of them, one can assume, had, like Hofstadter, published in the *AHR*.)

Meanwhile, having passed his comprehensive examinations, Hofstadter set out in quest of a dissertation topic. In a letter to his brother-in-law that typified Hofstadter's wry, self-deprecating sense of humor, he described the process. First, he considered writing a biography of "the old rascal Ben Wade" (the Radical Republican senator from Ohio), only to discover that Wade had destroyed most of his papers. Then he turned to Simon Cameron, Lincoln's first secretary of war, but abandoned that subject when he heard that "somebody from Indiana had been working on Cameron for 15 years." Columbia professor John A. Krout suggested a biography of Jeremiah Wadsworth, a colonial merchant who not only left abundant papers but had some admirers willing to help fund biographical research. Hofstadter, however, did not pursue the idea far—he and Felice considered Wadsworth inconsequential and kept referring to him as Jedediah Hockenpfuss. Finally, with Curti's approval, he settled on social Darwinism.[13] By mid-1940, he was hard at work, and two years later, at the precocious age of twenty-six, he completed the dissertation. *Social Darwinism in American Thought* was published by the University of Pennsylvania Press in 1944.

However serendipitous the process by which he found it, social Darwinism was the perfect subject for the young Hofstadter. It was a big topic, likely to interest a large audience, and it combined his growing interest in the history of social thought with his continuing alienation from American capitalism. It was the kind of subject, Felice wrote Harvey, "in which all his friends want to have a hand." "But in which they won't," Hofstadter added. The book focuses on the late nineteenth century and ends in 1915, the year before Hofstadter's birth. But, as he later observed, the "emotional resonances" that shaped his approach to the subject were those of his own youth, when conservatives used arguments descended from social Darwinism to justify resistance to radical political movements and government efforts to alleviate inequality. Studying social Darwinism helped explain "the disparity between our official individualism and the bitter facts of life as anyone could see them during the great depression."[14]

Social Darwinism in American Thought describes the broad impact on intellectual life of the scientific writings of Charles Darwin and the growing use of such Darwinian ideas as "natural selection," "survival of the fittest," and "the struggle for existence" to reinforce conservative, laissez-faire individualism. The book begins by tracing the conquest of Darwinian ideas among American scientists and liberal Protestant theologians, a conquest so complete that by the Gilded Age "every serious thinker felt obligated to reckon with" the implications of Darwin's writings. Hofstadter then examines the "vogue" of Herbert Spencer, the English philosopher who did more than any other individual to define nineteenth-century conservatism. Spencer, of course, preceded Darwin; well before the publication of *The Origin of Species,* Spencer not only coined the term "survival of the fittest" but developed a powerful critique of all forms of state interference with the "natural" workings of society, including regulation of business and public assistance to the poor. But Spencer's followers seized upon the authority of Darwin's work to claim scientific legitimacy for their outlook and to press home the analogy between the natural and social worlds, both of which, they claimed, evolved according to natural laws.

From Spencer, Hofstadter turns to a consideration of William Graham Sumner, the most influential American social Darwinist, whose writings glorified the competitive social order and justified existing social inequalities as the result of natural selection. Combining Darwinian ideas with the Protestant work ethic and classical economics, he condemned governmental activism, preferring instead a complete "abnegation of state power." Sumner offered defenders of the economic status quo a compelling rationale for opposing the demands of labor unions, Grangers, and others seeking to interfere with the "natural" functioning of the social order.

Despite the book's title and the deftness with which he sketches the lineaments of social Darwinism in its opening chapters, Hofstadter actually devotes more attention to the theory's critics than to its proponents. For a time, social Darwinism reigned supreme in American thought. But beginning in the 1880s, it came under attack from many sources—clergymen shocked by the inequities of the emerging industrial order and the harshness of unbridled competition, reformers proposing to unleash state activism in the service of social equality, and intellectuals of the emerging social sciences. Hofstadter makes no effort to disguise his distaste for the social Darwinists or his sympathy for the critics, especially the sociologists and philosophers who believed intellectuals could guide social progress (views extremely congenial to Hofstadter at the time he was writing). In the 1880s, sociologist Lester Ward pointed out that economic competition bred not simply individual advancement but giant new corporations whose economic might needed to be held in check by government, and he ridiculed the social Darwinists' "fundamental error" that "the favors of the world are distributed entirely according to merit." But Hofstadter's true heroes were the early-twentieth-century pragmatists. William James destroyed Spencer's hold on philosophical thought by pointing to the elements of psychology—sentiment, emotion, and so on—that were ignored in the Darwinian model and insisting that human intelligence enabled people to alter their own environment, thus rendering pointless the analogy with nature. James, however, evinced little interest in current events. Hofstadter identified more closely with John Dewey, whom he presents as a model of the socially responsible intellectual, the architect of a "new collectivism" in which an activist state attempts to guide and improve society.

By the turn of the century, social Darwinism was in full retreat. But even as Darwinian individualism waned, Darwinian ideas continued to influence social thinking in other ways. Rather than individuals striving for advancement, the struggling units of the analogy with nature become collectives— especially nations and races. With the United States emerging as a world power from the Spanish-American War, writers like John Fiske and Albert J. Beveridge marshaled Darwinian ideas in the service of imperialism, to legitimate the worldwide subordination of "inferior" races to Anglo-Saxon hegemony. In the eugenics movement that flourished in the early years of this century, Darwinism helped to underwrite the idea that immigration of less "fit" peoples was lowering the standard of American intelligence. Fortunately, the "racist-military" phase of social Darwinism was as thoroughly discredited by World War I, when it seemed uncomfortably akin to German militarism, as conservative individualism had been discredited by the attacks of progressive social scientists.

When Hofstadter tries to *explain* the rise and fall of social Darwinism, he falls back on the base-superstructure model shared by Marxists and Beardians in the 1930s. Hofstadter recognizes that there was nothing inevitable in the appropriation of Darwinism for conservative purposes. Marx, after all, was so impressed by *The Origin of Species*, which dethroned revealed religion and vindicated the idea of progress through ceaseless struggle (struggle among classes, in his reading, rather than individuals), that he proposed to dedicate *Capital* to Darwin— an honor the latter declined. How then to account for the ascendancy, until the 1890s, of individualist, laissez-faire Darwinism? The reason, Hofstadter writes, was that social Darwinism served the needs of those groups that controlled the "raw, aggressive, industrial society" of the Gilded Age. Spencer, Sumner, and the other social Darwinians were telling businessmen and political leaders what they wanted to hear. Subsequently, it was not merely the penetrating criticism of Ward, Dewey, and others but the middle class's growing disenchantment with unbridled competition, Hofstadter argues, that led it to repudiate social Darwinism and adopt a more reform-minded social outlook in the Progressive era.

Hofstadter's concluding thoughts amount to a reaffirmation both of the Beardian approach and of his own status as a radical intellectual. The rise and fall of social Darwinism, he writes, exemplified the "rule" that "changes in the structure of social ideas wait on general changes in economic and political life" and that ideas win wide acceptance based less on "truth and logic" than on their "suitability to the intellectual needs and preconceptions of social interests." This, he adds, was "one of the great difficulties that must be faced by rational strategists of social change." Clearly, Hofstadter still viewed economic self-interest as the basis of political action, and clearly he identified with those "rational strategists of social change" who hoped to move the nation beyond social Darwinism's legacy.

Actually, Hofstadter offered no independent analysis of either the structure of American society or of the ideas of most businessmen or politicians. His effort to explain social Darwinism's rise and fall is a kind of obiter dictum, largely confined to his brief concluding chapter. Indeed, Hofstadter later reflected that the book may have inadvertently encouraged the "intellectualist fallacy" by exaggerating the impact of ideas without placing them in the social context from which they sprang.[15] *Social Darwinism* is a work of intellectual history, not an examination of how ideas reflect economic structures. And as such, it retains much of its vitality half a century after it was written. The book's qualities would remain hallmarks of Hofstadter's subsequent writing—among them an amazing lucidity in presenting complex ideas, the ability to sprinkle his text with apt quotes that make precisely the right point, and the capacity to bring past individuals to life in telling portraits. For a dissertation, it is a work of remarkable range, drawing not only on the writings of sociologists and philosophers but also on novels, treatises, sermons, and popular magazines to explore the debates unleashed by Darwinism. Very much a product of a particular moment in American history, it transcends the particulars of its origins to offer a compelling portrait of a critical period in the development of American thought. To the end of his life, Hofstadter's writings would center on *Social Darwinism*'s underlying themes—the evolution of social thought, the social context of ideologies, and the role of ideas in politics.

Social Darwinism has had an impact matched by few books of its generation. Hofstadter did not invent the term *social Darwinism*, which originated in Europe in the 1880s and crossed the Atlantic in the early twentieth century. But before he wrote, it was used only on rare occasions; he made it a standard shorthand for a complex of late-nineteenth-century ideas, a familiar part of the lexicon of social thought. The book demonstrates Hofstadter's ability, even in a dissertation, to move beyond the academic readership to address a broad general public. Since its appearance in a revised paperback edition in 1955 (Hofstadter left the argument unchanged but added an author's note and made several hundred "purely stylistic" alterations), it has sold more than 200,000 copies.[16]

Although, thanks to Hofstadter, social Darwinism has earned a permanent place in the vocabulary of intellectual history, his analysis has not escaped criticism. While few scholars have challenged Hofstadter's account of the main currents of late-nineteenth-century American thought, some have cast doubt on the extent of Darwin's influence on both laissez-faire conservatives and their liberal and radical critics. Soon after Hofstadter's revised edition appeared, Irvin G. Wyllie published an influential essay disputing Darwin's impact on American businessmen. Entrepreneurs, he found, justified the accumulation of wealth not by appealing to a vision of ruthless competition in which the success of some meant the ruin of others but by reference to hard work, Christian philanthropy, and the conviction that the creation of wealth benefited society as a whole.[17]

Since Hofstadter had devoted little attention to businessmen, apart from Andrew Carnegie, Wyllie's findings did not significantly affect the book's main argument. More damaging was the criticism advanced by Robert C. Bannister, who argued that Hofstadter had greatly exaggerated Darwin's influence on social thinkers themselves.[18] Remarkably few late-nineteenth-century writers, Bannister found, either invoked Darwin's authority, referred directly to biological evolution, or used Darwinian terminology such as "survival of the fittest" and "the struggle for existence." The roots of their thought lay elsewhere, in classical economics and a preoccupation with defending property rights and limiting the power of the state. They were more likely to appeal to the authority of Adam Smith than to Darwin, more apt to be influenced by contemporary events such as the 1877 railroad strike than by analogies to biological evolution. In fact, Bannister concluded, social Darwinism existed mainly as an "epithet," a label devised by advocates of a reforming state to stigmatize laissez-faire conservatism.

Hofstadter, to be sure, never claimed that Darwin created Gilded Age individualism; rather, he wrote, Darwinian categories supplemented an existing vocabulary derived from laissez-faire economics. Moreover, Bannister's definition of social Darwinism, requiring explicit use of Darwinian language, ignores less direct influences on social thought and more subtle adaptations of scientific reasoning. Toward the end of his life, Hofstadter praised his critic for his careful reading of sources, but he went on to suggest that "intellectual history, even as made by men who try to be rational and who try to regard distinctions, proceeds by more gross distinctions than you are aware of." This was a fairly devastating critique of Bannister's approach (which, to his credit, Bannister included in the introduction to his own book).[19] Nonetheless, Bannister's basic point struck home. Today writers who examine Gilded Age conservatism are likely to locate its primary sources in realms other than Darwinism. Spencer's influence, it is true, still looms large; some have even suggested that the body of thought Hofstadter described ought to be called social Spencerism, not social Darwinism.[20]

This, however, would be a mistake, for if Hofstadter perhaps exaggerated Darwin's influence, he was certainly correct in identifying a commitment to developing a science of society as all but ubiquitous among late-nineteenth- and early-twentieth-century intellectuals. Darwin's writings helped to catalyze this commitment, which became a major point of self-definition and self-justification for intellectuals at a time when, through the rise of social science, their role in American society was becoming institutionalized. Hofstadter's central insight—that analogies with science helped to shape the way Americans perceived and interpreted issues from the differences between races and classes to the implications of state intervention in the economy—remains the starting point for serious investigations of American thought during the Gilded Age.[21]

Inevitably, *Social Darwinism* now seems in some ways dated. Today, in the wake of the "new social history," historians are more cognizant of the many groups that make up American society and no longer write confidently, as Hofstadter did, of a single "public mind." But the most striking difference between Hofstadter's cast of mind and that of our own time lies in his resolute conviction that social Darwinism was an unfortunate but thankfully closed chapter in the history of social thought. Hofstadter wrote from the certainty that social Darwinism was demonstrably wrong, that biological analogies are "utterly use-less" in understanding human society, and that this episode had all been some kind of "ghastly mistake."

"A resurgence of social Darwinism . . . ," Hofstadter did note, "was always a possibility so long as there is a strong ele-ment of predacity in society." But he could hardly have fore-seen the resurrection in the 1980s and 1990s of biological explanations for human development[22] and of the social Dar-winist mentality, if not the name itself: that government should not intervene to affect the "natural" workings of the economy, that the distribution of rewards within society reflects individual merit rather than historical circumstances, and that the plight of the less fortunate, whether individuals or races, arises from their own failings. Had he lived to see social Darwinism's recrudescence, Hofstadter would certainly have noted how two previously distinct strands of this ideology have merged in today's conservatism—the laissez-faire individualism of a William Graham Sumner (who, it should be noted, condemned the imperial state with the same vigor he applied to government intervention in the economy) and the militarist and racist Darwinism of the early twentieth century.

If *Social Darwinism* announced Hofstadter as one of the most promising scholars of his generation, his second work, *The American Political Tradition*, published in 1948, propelled him to the very forefront of his profession.[23] Since its appearance, this brilliant series of portraits of prominent Americans from the founding fathers through Jefferson, Jackson, Lincoln, and FDR has been a standard work in both college and high school history classes and has been read by millions outside the academy. Hofstadter's insight was that virtually all his subjects held essentially the same underlying beliefs. Instead of persistent conflict (whether between agrarians and industrialists, capital and labor, or Democrats and Republicans), American history was characterized by broad agreement on fundamentals, particularly the virtues of individual liberty, private property, and capitalist enterprise. In *Social Darwinism*, he had observed that Spencer's doctrines came to America "long after individualism had become a national tradition." Now he appeared to be saying that the subject of his first book *was* the American political tradition.

With its emphasis on the ways an ideological consensus had shaped American development, *The American Political Tradition* in many ways marked Hofstadter's break with the Beardian and Marxist traditions. Along with Daniel Boorstin's *The Genius of American Politics* and Louis Hartz's *The Liberal Tradition in America* (both published a few years afterward), Hofstadter's second book came to be seen as the foundation of the "consensus history" of the 1950s. But Hofstadter's writing never devolved into the uncritical celebration of the American experience that characterized much "consensus" writing. As Arthur Schlesinger, Jr., observed in a 1969 essay, there was a basic difference between *The American Political Tradition* and works like Boorstin's: "For Hofstadter [and, Schlesinger might have added, Hartz] perceived the consensus from a radical perspective, from the outside, and deplored it; while Boorstin perceived it from the inside and celebrated it." As a courtesy, Schlesinger sent Hofstadter a draft of the essay. In the margin opposite this sentence, Hofstadter, who never felt entirely comfortable with the consensus label, scribbled "Thank you."[24]

Hofstadter had abandoned Beard's analysis of American development, but he retained his mentor's iconoclastic, debunking spirit. In Hofstadter's hands, Jefferson became a political chameleon, Jackson an exponent of liberal capitalism, Lincoln a mythmaker, and Roosevelt a pragmatic opportunist. And the domination of individualism and capitalism in American life produced not a benign freedom from "European" ideological conflicts, but a form of intellectual and political bankruptcy, an inability to think in original ways about the modern world. If the book has a hero, it is abolitionist Wendell Phillips, the only figure in *The American Political Tradition* never to hold political office. As in *Social Darwinism*, Hofstadter seemed to identify most of all with the engaged reformist intellectual. It is indeed ironic that one of the most devastating indictments of American political culture ever written should have become the introduction to American history for two generations of students. One scholar at the time even sought to develop an alternative book of essays on America's greatest presidents precisely in order to counteract the "confusion and disillusionment" he feared Hofstadter was sowing among undergraduates.[25]

"All my books," Hofstadter wrote in the 1960s, "have been, in a certain sense, topical in their inspiration. That is to say, I have always begun with a concern with some present reality." His first two books, he went on, "refract the experiences of the depression era and the New Deal."[26] In the 1950s, a different "reality" shaped Hofstadter's writing—the cold war and McCarthyism. Having remarried after the death of his first wife in 1945, Hofstadter assumed a teaching position at Columbia and again found himself part of New York's intellectual world. But this was very different from the radical days of the 1930s. He had "grown a great deal more conservative in the past few years," Hofstadter wrote Merle Curti, then teaching at Wisconsin, in 1953.[27] Unlike many New York intellectuals, including a number of his friends, Hofstadter never made a career of anticommunism. Nor did he embrace neoconservatism, join the Congress for Cultural Freedom, or become an uncritical apologist for the cold war. He was repelled by McCarthyism (although he declined Curti's invitation to condemn publicly the firing of communist professors at the University of Washington).[28] After supporting with "immense enthusiasm" Adlai Stevenson's campaign for the White House in 1952, Hofstadter retreated altogether from politics. "I can no longer describe myself as a radical, though I don't consider

myself to be a conservative either," he wrote Harvey Swados
a decade after Stevenson's defeat. "I suppose the truth is, although my interests are still very political, I none the less have
no politics."[29]

What Hofstadter did have was a growing sense of the fra-
gility of intellectual freedom and social comity. His next book
was *The Development of Academic Freedom in the United States,* written
in collaboration with his Columbia colleague Walter P. Metzger
and published in 1955. As with other intellectuals, his sensibility was strongly reinforced by the Holocaust in Europe and
the advent of McCarthyism at home. Hofstadter understood
McCarthyism not as a thrust for political advantage among
conservatives seeking to undo the legacy of the New Deal but
as the outgrowth of a deep-seated anti-intellectualism and
provincialism in the American population. The result was to
reinforce a distrust of mass politics that had been simmering
ever since he left the Communist party in 1939. This attitude
was reinforced by his search for new ways of understanding
political behavior. Reared on the assumption that politics essentially reflects economic interest, he now became fascinated with
alternative explanations of political conduct—status anxieties,
irrational hatreds, paranoia. Influenced by the popularity of
Freudianism among New York intellectuals of the 1950s and by
his close friendships with the sociologist C. Wright Mills and
literary critics Lionel Trilling and Alfred Kazin, Hofstadter
became more and more sensitive to the importance of symbolic
conduct, unconscious motivation, and, as he wrote in *The Age of
Reform* (1955), the "complexities in our history which our conventional images of the past have not yet caught."

Hofstadter applied these insights to the history of American
political culture in a remarkable series of books that made plain

his growing conservatism and his sense of alienation from what he called America's periodic "fits of moral crusading." *The Age of Reform* offered an interpretation of populism and progressivism "from the perspective of our own time." In his master's essay, Hofstadter had thoroughly sympathized with the struggles of the South's downtrodden tenant farmers. Now, he portrayed the populists of the late nineteenth century as small entrepreneurs standing against the inevitable tide of economic development. He saw them as taking refuge in a nostalgic agrarian myth or lashing out against imagined enemies from British bankers to Jews, in a precursor to "modern authoritarian movements." (Interestingly, this interpretation still bore the mark of the traditional Marxist critique of petty-bourgeois social movements; the American Marxist thinker Daniel DeLeon had said much the same thing in the 1890s.)

In *Social Darwinism*, William Graham Sumner and the capitalist plutocracy of the Gilded Age had emerged as the main threats to American democracy; while noting the underside of progressivism—its racism and Anglo-Saxonism—Hofstadter seemed to embrace its demand for state activism against social injustice. In *The Age of Reform,* he depicted the progressives as a displaced bourgeoisie seeking in political reform a way to overcome their decline in status. Rather than a precursor of the New Deal, as it was commonly seen, progressivism, with its infatuation with the idea of pure democracy, was the source of some of "our most troublesome contemporary delusions" about politics. A similar sensibility informed Hofstadter's next two books. In *Anti-Intellectualism in American Life* (1963), he identified an American heartland "filled with people who are often fundamentalist in religion, nativist in prejudice, isolationist in foreign policy, and conservative in economics" as a persistent danger to intellectual life. In *The Paranoid Style in American Politics* (1965), he suggested that a common irrationality characterized popular enthusiasms of both the right and the left throughout American history.

The Age of Reform and *Anti-Intellectualism* won Hofstadter his two Pulitzer Prizes, but ironically today both seem more dated than his earlier books. Their deep distrust of mass politics, their apparent dismissal of the substantive basis of reform movements, strike the reader, even in today's conservative climate, as exaggerated and elitist. And since the rise of the "new social history," it has become impossible to study mass movements without immersing oneself in local primary sources, rather than relying on the kind of imaginative reading of published works at which Hofstadter excelled. These books seemed to wed him to a consensus vision that deemed the American political system fundamentally sound and its critics essentially irrational.

Hofstadter's, however, was too protean an intellect to remain satisfied for long with the consensus framework. As social turmoil engulfed the country in the mid-1960s, Hofstadter remained as prolific as ever, but his underlying assumptions shifted again. In *The Progressive Historians* (1968), he attempted to come to terms once and for all with Beard and his generation. Their portrait of an America racked by perennial conflict, he noted, was overdrawn, but by the same token, the consensus outlook could hardly explain the American Revolution, the Civil War, or other key periods of discord in the nation's past (including, by implication, the 1960s). *American Violence* (1970), a documentary volume edited with his graduate student Michael Wallace, offered a chilling record of political and social turbulence that utterly contradicted the consensus vision of a nation placidly evolving without serious disagreements. Finally, in *America at 1750*, the first volume in a proposed three-part narrative history of the nation, Hofstadter offered a portrait that brilliantly took account of the paradoxical coexistence of individual freedom and opportunity and widespread social injustice and human bondage in the colonial era. The book remained unfinished at the time of his death from leukemia in 1970, offering only a tantalizing suggestion of what his full account of the American past might have been.

For all his accomplishments, Hofstadter was utterly without pretension, always unintimidating, and never too busy to talk about one's work. He did not try to impose his own interests or views on his students—far from it. If no "Hofstadter school" emerged from Columbia, it is because he had no desire to create one. Indeed, it often seemed during the 1960s that his graduate students, many of whom were actively involved in the civil rights and antiwar movements, were having as much influence on his evolving interests and outlook as he was on theirs.

It would not be strictly true to call Hofstadter a great teacher. Writing was his passion, and he did not share the love of the classroom that marks the truly exceptional instructor. Hofstadter disliked the lecture podium intensely and almost seemed to go out of his way to make his lectures unappealing, perhaps to drive away some of the large numbers who inevitably registered for his courses. He was at his best in small seminars and individual consultations and when criticizing written work. Here his erudition, open-mindedness, and desire to help each student do the best work of which he or she was capable came to the fore.

Despite his death at the relatively young age of fifty-four, Hofstadter left a prolific body of work, remarkable for its originality and readability and his capacity to range over the length and breadth of American history. From *Social Darwinism* to *America at 1750*, his writings stand as a model of what historical scholarship at its finest can aspire to achieve.

PART II

RETHINKING HISTORY IN A CHANGING WORLD

THREE

AMERICAN FREEDOM IN A GLOBAL AGE

For my presidential address to the American Historical Association's annual meeting in January 2001, I chose to discuss how scholars might take the current preoccupation with globalization as an opportunity to think in new ways about aspects of the American past, particularly the idea of freedom and how its evolution has been shaped in part by this country's interaction with the larger world.

•

At this first AHA meeting of the twenty-first century, it is worthwhile to turn our attention briefly to the last fin de siècle. One hundred years ago, the United States had just emerged victorious in its "splendid little war" against Spain. It was actively engaged in the decidedly less splendid struggle to subdue the movement for independence in the Philippines. Both conflicts announced that the country was poised to take its place among the world's great powers, and writers here and abroad confidently predicted that American influence would soon span the globe. The precise nature of that influence was a matter of some dispute. In his 1902 book *The New Empire*, Brooks Adams, whose brother Charles Francis Adams served as this association's president exactly one century ago, saw America's rise to world power as essentially economic. "As the United States becomes an imperial market," he proclaimed, "she stretches out along the trade-routes which lead from foreign countries to her heart, as every empire has stretched out from the days of Sargon to our own." Within fifty years, Adams predicted, "the United States will outweigh any single empire, if not all empires combined."[1]

The year 1902 also witnessed a prediction with a somewhat different emphasis, offered by W. T. Stead in a short volume with the arresting title *The Americanisation of the World: or, The Trend of the Twentieth Century*. Stead was a sensationalist English editor whose previous writings included an exposé of London prostitution, *Maiden Tribute to Modern Babylon*. He would later meet his death as a passenger on the *Titanic*. Convinced that the United States was emerging as "the greatest of world-powers," Stead proposed that it and his homeland "merge" (by which he meant both political union and individual intermarriages), so that the enervated British could have their "exhausted excheq-uer" revived by an infusion of America's "exuberant energies." But what was most striking about Stead's little essay was that he located the essential source of American power less in the realm of military or economic might than in the relentless international spread of American culture—art, music, journalism, theater, even ideas about religion and gender relations. He foresaw a future in which the United States would promote its values and interests through an unending involvement in the affairs of other nations.[2]

Today we are in many ways living in the world Adams and Stead imagined (although Britain does retain its nominal independence). At the dawn of the twenty-first century, the United States is indisputably the world's preeminent military, economic, and cultural power. Moreover, the flow of people, investment, production, culture, and communications across national boundaries that impressed both Adams and Stead continues its rapid growth. We are constantly being reminded that the world we inhabit is becoming smaller and more integrated and that formerly autonomous nations are bound ever more tightly by a complex web of economic and cultural connections. Globalization, the popular shorthand term for these processes, has been called "*the* concept of the 1990s." Its novelty, extent, and consequences, however, remain subjects of heated disagreement. Is globalization producing a homogenized and "Americanized" world, a unified global culture whose economic arrangements, social values, and political institutions are based primarily on those of the United States? Or is it transforming societies without making them identical, producing "multiple modernities" in which international images and commodities are incorporated locally in a continuing process of selection and reinterpretation?[3]

I do not plan tonight to try to answer these questions, which now engage the attention of some of our most prominent social scientists. But as a historian, I feel it necessary to point out that like every other product of human activity, globalization itself has a history. The dream of global unity goes back to the days of Alexander the Great and Genghis Khan. The internationalization of commerce and culture and the reshuffling of the world's peoples have been going on for centuries. Today's globalized communications follow in the footsteps of clipper ships, the telegraph, and the telephone. Today's international movements for social change—including protests against some of the adverse consequences of globalization— have their precedents in transnational labor and socialist movements, religious revivals, and struggles against slavery and for women's rights. As for economic globalization, Karl Marx long ago pointed out that capitalism is an international system that "must nestle everywhere, settle everywhere, establish connections everywhere." This was why he and Friedrich Engels called upon proletarians to unite as a global force. "All old-established national industries," they wrote, "have been destroyed or are daily being destroyed. . . . In place of the old local and national seclusion and self-sufficiency, we have intercourse in every direction, universal interdependence of nations." These words were written in 1848.[4]

Nonetheless, the dimensions and speed of globalization have certainly accelerated in the last two decades. And by remaking our present, globalization invites us to rethink our past. All history, as the saying goes, is contemporary history. Today our heightened awareness of globalization—however the term is delimited and defined—should challenge historians to become more cognizant of how past events are embedded in an international, even a global context. Nearly fifty years ago, Geoffrey Barraclough wondered whether histories with a "myopic concentration on individual nations" could effectively illuminate "the world in which we live."[5] For American historians, this question is even more pertinent today.

The institutions, processes, and values that have shaped American history—from capitalism to political democracy, slavery, and consumer culture—arose out of global processes and can be understood only in an international context. This, of course, is hardly a new insight. Back in the 1930s, W.E.B. Du Bois insisted that it was impossible to understand the black experience in the United States without reference to "that dark and vast sea of human labor in China and India, the South Seas and all Africa . . . that great majority of mankind, on whose bent and broken backs rest today the founding stones of modern industry." Herbert E. Bolton warned that by treating the American past in isolation, historians were helping to raise up a "nation of chauvinists."[6]

At the time, these pleas more or less fell on deaf ears. But some of the best recent works of American history have developed complex understandings of the nation's relationship to the larger world. The emerging "Atlantic" perspective on the colonial era offers the promise of seeing early American history not simply as an offshoot of Great Britain or as a prelude to the Revolution but as part and parcel of the international expansion of European empires and the transatlantic migration of peoples. Bonnie Anderson's history of the "first international women's movement" traces the transatlantic exchange of ideas on issues ranging from suffrage to childrearing and divorce. *Barbarian Virtues*, by Matthew Jacobson, examines how a century ago Americans' real and imagined encounters with foreign peoples—as potential customers and laborers, and as exemplars of a "lower" state of civilization—helped shape a new sense of national identity. Daniel Rodgers's *Atlantic Crossings* demonstrates that American progressivism must be seen as part of an international discussion about "social politics."

Important writings in economic history stress how world markets have shaped our agriculture, port cities, and industrial towns. Most of these works focus on relationships between the United States and Europe. But the best recent work in Asian-American studies has begun to develop what might be called a Pacific perspective that moves beyond an older paradigm based on immigration and assimilation to examine how continuing transnational cultural and economic interactions shape the experience of minority groups within the United States. Yet in nearly all areas of American history, such works remain dwarfed by those that stop at the nation's borders.[7]

A little over a decade ago, my predecessor as AHA president Akira Iriye called for historians to "internationalize" the study of history by treating the entire world as their framework of study. This is a daunting challenge, probably impossible for most historians to accomplish. Of course, as Professor Iriye well knows, histories based on international paradigms—"the West," "modernization," the "Judeo-Christian tradition"—can be every bit as obfuscating as histories that are purely national. My point is somewhat different—that even histories organized along the lines of the nation-state must be, so to speak, de-provincialized, placed in the context of international interactions. Since the birth of the modern era, the nation has constituted the principal framework for historical study. It is likely to remain so for the foreseeable future. Internationalizing history does not mean abandoning or homogenizing national histories, dissolving the experience of the United States, or any other nation, in a sea of supranational processes. International dynamics operate in different ways in different countries. Every nation, to one extent or another, thinks of itself

as exceptional—a conviction, of course, rather more prominent in the United States (and among its historians) than elsewhere. But globalization does force us to think about history in
somewhat different ways.[8]

Historians are fully aware of how American military might,
commodities, and culture have affected the rest of the world,
especially in the twentieth century. We know how the United
States has exported everything from Coca-Cola to ideas about
democracy and "free enterprise." Far less attention has been
devoted to how our history has been affected from abroad.
"Europe," Frantz Fanon wrote in *The Wretched of the Earth*,
"is literally the creation of the Third World."[9] Fanon was referring not only to the wealth Europe gleaned from its colonial
dependencies but to the fact that the encounters of different peoples—real encounters and those of the imagination—
crystallize political ideologies and concepts of identity. They
also, one might add, always seem to produce inequalities of
power and of rights. Fanon's insight needs to be extended to
the United States. An understanding of America cannot be
obtained purely from within America. To illustrate my point, I
want to refer to the most central idea in American political culture, an idea that anchors the American sense of exceptional
national identity: freedom.

No idea is more fundamental to Americans' sense of themselves as individuals or as a nation than freedom. The central
term in our political vocabulary, *freedom*—or *liberty*, with which
it is almost always used interchangeably—is deeply embedded
in the record of our history and the language of everyday life.
The Declaration of Independence lists liberty among mankind's inalienable rights; the Constitution announces as its

purpose to secure liberty's blessings. Obviously, other peoples also cherish freedom, but the idea does seem to occupy a more prominent place in public and private discourse in the United States than elsewhere. The ubiquitous American expression "It's a free country," invoked by disobedient children and assertive adults to explain or justify their actions, is not, I believe, familiar in other societies. "Every man in the street, white, black, red or yellow," wrote the educator and statesman Ralph Bunche in 1940, "knows that this is 'the land of the free' . . . 'the cradle of liberty.'"[10]

In *The Story of American Freedom*, published in 1998, while not entirely neglecting the international dimensions of American history, I emphasized how the changing meaning of freedom has been shaped and reshaped by social and political struggles within the United States—battles, for example, over the abolition of slavery, women's rights, labor organization, and freedom of speech for those outside the social mainstream.[11] Yet America's relationship, real and imagined, with the rest of the world has also powerfully influenced the idea of freedom and its evolution. As with other central elements of our political language—independence, equality, and citizenship, for example—freedom has been defined and redefined with reference to its putative opposite. The most striking example, of course, is slavery, a stark homegrown illustration of the nature of unfreedom that helped to define Americans' language of liberty in the colonial era and well into the nineteenth century. In the early labor movement's crusade against "wage slavery" and denunciations of "the slavery of sex" by advocates of women's rights, the condition of African-Americans powerfully affected how free Americans understood their own situation.

While Americans have frequently identified threats to freedom at home, including slavery, luxury, and a too-powerful federal government, they have also looked abroad to locate dangers to freedom. The American Revolution was inspired, in part, by the conviction that Great Britain was conspiring to eradicate freedom in North America. In the twentieth century, world affairs have frequently been understood as titanic struggles between a "free world," centered in the United States, and its enemies—Nazis during World War II, communists during the cold war, and most recently "terrorists," drug cartels, or Islamic fundamentalists.

Of course, the relationship between American freedom and the outside world works both ways. "America," as myth and reality, has for centuries played a part in how other peoples think about their own societies. The United States has frequently been viewed from abroad as the embodiment of one or another kind of freedom. European labor, in the nineteenth century, identified this country as a land where working men and women enjoyed freedoms not available in the Old World. In the twentieth, younger generations throughout the world selectively appropriated artifacts of American popular culture for acts of cultural rebellion. Some foreign observers, to be sure, have taken a rather jaundiced view of Americans' stress on their own liberty. The "tyranny of the majority," Alexis de Tocqueville commented, ruled the United States: "I know of no country, in which there is so little independence of mind and real freedom of discussion as in America." A century and a half later, another French writer, Jean Baudrillard, concluded his own tour of the United States with the observation that if New York and Los Angeles now stood "at the center of the world," it is a world defined not so much by freedom as by "wealth, power, senility, indifference, puritanism and mental hygiene, poverty and waste, technological futility and aimless violence."[12]

My interest here, however, is not images of America emanating from abroad or the global impact of the United States, but how global embeddedness has affected American history itself. At key moments in our history, America's relationship to the outside world has helped to establish how freedom is understood within the United States. To a considerable degree, the self-definition of the United States as a nation-state with a special mission to bring freedom to all mankind depends on the "otherness" of the outside world, often expressed in the Manichean categories of New World versus Old or free world versus slave.

The idea of America as an embodiment of freedom in a world overrun by tyranny goes back to well before the American Revolution. Ironically, however, this ideology must be understood not simply with reference to the unique conditions of North American settlement—available land, weak government, and so on—but as a conscious creation of European policymakers. From the earliest days of settlement, migrants from Britain and the Continent held the promise of the New World to be liberation from the social inequalities and widespread economic dependence of the Old. Many others saw America as a divinely appointed locale where man could, for the first time, be truly free in the sense of worshiping God in a manner impossible in Europe. But these ideas can be understood only in the context of the clash of empires that produced American settlement in the first place and that engaged the colonists in a seemingly endless series of wars involving the rival French, Spanish, and Dutch empires. British monarchs did as much as colonists themselves to create the idea of America as an asylum for "those whom bigots chase from foreign lands" by actively encouraging continental emigration to the New World in order to strengthen their colonies without depleting the population of the British Isles. As Marilyn C. Baseler writes, colonial liberty of conscience "was largely a byproduct of English policies and did not necessarily reflect a strong commitment by America's early settlers to the principles of religious freedom."[13]

The growth of the three most dynamic empires of the eighteenth century—the British, French, and Dutch—depended on the debasement of millions of people into slavery and the dispossession of millions of native inhabitants of the Americas. The yoking of freedom and domination was a global phenomenon, intrinsic to the imperial expansion of Europe, England's mainland colonies not excepted. Nonetheless, all three empires developed discourses claiming a special relationship to freedom (partly in contrast to the Spanish, who were seen as representing tyranny at home and a peculiarly inhumane form of imperialism overseas). From an international perspective, claims by Britain and her colonies to a unique relationship with liberty ring somewhat hollow. The Dutch actually had more justification in claiming to represent the principle of religious toleration, while France respected the principle of "free air"—which liberated any slave setting foot on metropolitan soil—well before Great Britain. Nonetheless, the idea that the Anglo-American world enjoyed a unique measure of freedom was widely disseminated in the colonies. Belief in freedom as the common heritage of all Britons was, Jack P. Greene writes, the "single most important element in defining a larger Imperial identity for Britain and the British Empire." It served to cast imperial wars against Catholic France and Spain as struggles between liberty and tyranny, a language in which to this day virtually every American war has been described.[14]

The coming of independence rendered the rights of "free-born Englishmen" irrelevant in America. But the Revolution did more than substitute one parochial ideology of freedom for another. The struggle for independence universalized the idea of American freedom. Even before 1776, patriotic orators and pamphleteers were identifying America as a special place with a special mission, "a land of liberty, the seat of virtue, the asylum of the oppressed, a name and a praise in the whole earth," to quote Joseph Warren. This vision required a somewhat exaggerated negative image of the rest of the world. Outside British North America, proclaimed Samuel Williams in *A Discourse on the Love of Our Country* (1775), mankind was sunk in debauchery and despotism. In Asia and Africa, "the very idea of liberty" was "unknown." Even in Europe, Williams claimed, the "vital flame" of "freedom" was being extinguished. Here, and here alone, was "the country of free men."[15]

This sense of American uniqueness was pervasive in the revolutionary era, as was the view of the Revolution as not simply an internal squabble within the British Empire but the opening of a new era in human history. The point was not necessarily to spark liberation movements in other countries but to highlight the alleged differences between the United States and the rest of mankind. One pamphleteer of 1776, Ebenezer Baldwin, predicted that even in the year 2000 America would remain the world's sole center of freedom. But while affirming their uniqueness, Americans from the outset were obsessed with the repute in which they were held abroad. George Washington defended the suppression of the Whiskey Rebellion, in part, because of "the impression it will make on *others*"—the others being European skeptics who wished to see the world-historical experiment fail because they did not believe human beings could "govern ourselves." Over half a century later, Abraham Lincoln would contend that slavery weakened the American mission by exposing the country to the charge of hypocrisy from the "enemies of free institutions" abroad.[16]

In his *History of the American Revolution* (1789), David Ramsay, the father of American historical writing, insisted that what defined the new nation was not the usual bases of nationality— a set of boundaries, a long-established polity, or a common "race" or ethnicity—but a special destiny "to enlarge the happiness of mankind." This narrative was elaborated by nineteenth-century historians such as Walter H. Prescott, Francis Parkman, and George Bancroft. In their account, the seeds of liberty, planted in Puritan New England, had reached their inevitable flowering in the American Revolution and westward expansion. These writers were fully aware of the global dimension of American history, but their conviction that the United States represented a unique embodiment of the idea of freedom inevitably fostered a certain insularity. Since territorial growth meant "extending the area of freedom," those who stood in the way—European powers with legal title to part of the North American continent, Native Americans, Mexicans— were by definition obstacles to the progress of liberty. In the outlook of most white Americans, the West was not a battleground of peoples and governments but an "empty" space ready to be occupied as part of the divine mission of the United States.[17]

American expansion, which involved constant encounters with nonwhite people (or people, like the Mexicans, defined as nonwhite), greatly enhanced what might be called the exclusionary dimensions of American freedom. The nation's rapid territorial growth was widely viewed as evidence of the innate superiority of a mythical construct known as the "Anglo-Saxon race," whose special qualities made it uniquely suited to bring freedom and prosperity to the continent and the world. America may have been an empire, but in Thomas Jefferson's phrase, it was an "empire of liberty," supposedly distinct from the oppressive empires of Europe.[18]

Of course, the contradiction between the rhetoric of universal liberty and the actual limits of freedom within the United States goes back to the era of colonization. The slavery controversy was primarily a matter internal to the United States. But as an institution that existed throughout the Western hemisphere, and whose abolition was increasingly demanded by a movement transcending national boundaries, slavery's impact on American freedom had an international dimension as well. Slavery did much to determine how a nation born in revolution reacted to revolutions abroad. American culture in the antebellum period glorified the revolutionary heritage. But acceptable revolutions were those made by white men—like the Greeks or Hungarians—seeking their freedom from tyrannical government, not those made by slaves rebelling against their own lack of liberty. Denmark Vesey and Nat Turner were not part of the pantheon of national heroes, nor was Toussaint L'Ouverture greeted with the same enthusiasm as Louis Kossuth. Indeed, unlike the French, whose revolution certainly had its share of violence, the carnage in Saint-Domingue was taken to demonstrate that blacks lacked the capacity for self-government—in a word, that they were congenitally unfit for the enjoyment of freedom.[19]

As the nineteenth century wore on, the centrality of slavery to American life exposed the nation to the charge of willful hypocrisy, and from no quarter was the charge more severe than from blacks themselves. Black abolitionists were among the most penetrating critics of the hollowness of official pronouncements about American freedom. In calling for a redefinition of freedom as an entitlement of all mankind, not one from which certain groups defined as "races" could legitimately be excluded, black abolitionists repudiated the rhetorical division of the world into the United States, a beacon of freedom, and the Old World, a haven of oppression. "I am ashamed," declared black abolitionist William Wells Brown, "when I hear men talking about . . . the despotism of Napoleon III. . . . Before you boast of your freedom and Christianity, do your duty to your fellow man."[20]

Most strikingly, abolitionists, black and white alike, reversed the familiar dichotomy between American freedom and British tyranny. Once slavery had been abolished in the British Empire, the former mother country represented freedom more genuinely than the United States. August 1, the anniversary of emancipation in the British West Indies, became the black Fourth of July, the occasion of annual "freedom celebrations" that pointedly drew attention to the distinction between the "monarchial liberty" of a nation that had abolished slavery and "republican slavery" in the United States. With the passage in 1850 of the Fugitive Slave Act, several thousand black Americans fled to Canada, fearing reenslavement in the United States. Which country was now the asylum of the oppressed?[21]

As Linda Colley has argued, the abolition of slavery in 1833 enabled Britons to regain the earlier sense of their own nation as a paradigm of freedom. Emancipation demonstrated Britain's superior national virtue compared to the United States and gave it, despite the sordid realities of British imperialism, an irrefutable claim to moral integrity. A similar process occurred in the United States. After decades of the slavery controversy, which had somewhat tarnished the sense of a special American mission to preserve and promote liberty, the Civil War and emancipation reinforced the identification of the United States with the progress of freedom, linking this mission as never before with the power of the national state. By the 1880s, James Bryce was struck by the strength not only of Americans' commitment to freedom but of their conviction that they were the "only people" truly to enjoy it.[22]

If, in the nineteenth century, America's encounter with the world beyond the Western hemisphere had been more ideological, as it were, than material, the twentieth saw the country emerge as a continuous and powerful actor on a global stage. At key moments of worldwide involvement, the encounter with a foreign "other" subtly affected the meaning of freedom in the United States. One such episode was the struggle against Nazi Germany, which not only highlighted concern with aspects of American freedom that had previously been neglected but fundamentally transformed perceptions of who was entitled to enjoy the blessings of liberty in the United States. It also gave birth to a powerful rhetoric, the division of the planet into a "free world" and an unfree world that would long outlive the defeat of Adolf Hitler.

Even before the United States entered World War II, the gathering confrontation with Nazism helped to promote a broadened awareness of civil liberties as a central element of American freedom. Today, when asked to define their rights as citizens, Americans instinctively turn to the privileges enumerated in the Bill of Rights—freedom of speech, the press, and religion, for example. But for many decades, the social and legal defenses of free expression were extremely fragile in the United States. A broad rhetorical commitment to this ideal coexisted with stringent restrictions on speech that was deemed radical or obscene. It was only in 1939 that the Department of Justice established its Civil Liberties Unit, for the first time in American history, according to Attorney General Frank Murphy, placing "the full weight of the department . . . behind the effort to preserve in this country the blessings of liberty."[23]

There were many causes for this development, from a revulsion against the severe repression of the World War I era to a new awareness in the 1930s of restraints on free speech by opponents of labor organizing. But what Michael Kammen calls the "discovery" of the Bill of Rights on the eve of America's entry into World War II owed much to the ideological struggle against Nazism and the invocation of freedom as a shorthand way of describing the myriad differences between American and German society and politics. Once the country entered World War II, the Nazi counterexample was frequently cited by defenders of civil liberties in the United States. Freedom of speech took its place as one of the "four essential human freedoms," President Franklin D. Roosevelt's description of Allied war aims. Not only did the Four Freedoms embody the "crucial difference" between the Allies and their enemies, but in the future, Roosevelt promised, they would be enjoyed "everywhere in the world," an updating of the centuries-old vision of America instructing the rest of mankind in the enjoyment of liberty.[24]

Talk of freedom permeated wartime America—in advertisements, films, publications of the Office of War Information, and in Roosevelt's own rhetoric. Over and over Roosevelt described the war as a titanic battle between "freedom" and "slavery." The Free World, a term popularized in 1940–41 by those pressing for American intervention in the European conflict, assumed a central role in wartime rhetoric. It was in a speech to the Free World Association in 1942 that Vice President Henry Wallace outlined his vision of a global New Deal emerging from the war, in which the nation's involvement in the postwar world would universalize the Four Freedoms and ensure the promise of the American Revolution. Wallace was, in part, responding to Henry Luce's more chauvinistic call for the United States to assume the role of "dominant power in the world." But whatever their differences in outlook, both Wallace and Luce envisioned the United States as henceforth promoting freedom not merely by example or occasional international intervention but via an unending involvement in the affairs of other nations. Indeed, at the war's end, globalist language and imagery pervaded the mass media, and the idea that America had inherited a global responsibility evoked remarkably little dissent.[25]

If World War II presaged a transformation, in the name of freedom, of the country's traditional relationship with the rest of the world, it also reshaped Americans' understanding of the internal boundaries of freedom. The struggle against Nazi tyranny and its theory of a master race discredited ideas of inborn ethnic and racial inequality and gave a new impetus to the long-denied struggle for racial justice at home. A pluralist definition of American society, in which all citizens enjoyed equally the benefits of freedom, had been pioneered in the 1930s by leftists and liberals associated with the Popular Front.

It became the government's official stance during the Second World War. What set the United States apart from its wartime foes was not simply dedication to the ideals of the Four Freedoms but the resolve that these should extend to persons of all races, religions, and national origins. It was during the war that a shared American Creed of freedom, equality, and ethnic and religious "brotherhood" came to be seen as the foundation of national unity. Racism was the enemy's philosophy; intolerance was a foreign import, not a homegrown product.[26]

Reading American pluralism backward into history, postwar scholars made the American Creed a timeless definition of American nationality, ignoring the powerful ethnic and racial strains in the actual history of our national consciousness. At the same time, however, the rise of anticolonial movements in Africa and Asia inspired the rapid growth of what would later be called a "diasporic" consciousness among black Americans, which highlighted the deeply rooted racial inequalities in the United States and insisted they could be understood only through the prism of imperialism's long global history. Like many other products of the war years, this vision of racial inequality in the United States as part of a global system rather than as a maladjustment between American ideals and behavior did not long survive the advent of the cold war.[27]

Rhetorically, the cold war was in many ways a continuation of the battles of World War II. The discourse of a world sharply divided into opposing camps, one representing freedom and the other slavery, was reinvigorated in the worldwide struggle against communism. Once again the United States was the leader of a global crusade for freedom against a demonic, ideologically driven antagonist. Among other things, the cold war was a crucible in which postwar liberalism was reformulated. A revulsion against both Nazism and communism abroad, reinforced by the excesses of McCarthyism at home, propelled liberal thinkers toward a wholesale repudiation of ideological mass politics. In its place emerged a pragmatic, managerial liberalism meant to protect democratic institutions against excesses of the popular will.

The debate over communism helps explain the widespread impact, at least among liberal intellectuals, of Sir Isaiah Berlin's 1958 essay "Two Concepts of Liberty." Berlin distinguished sharply between "negative liberty"—the absence of external obstacles to the fulfillment of one's desires—and "positive liberty," which led to the subordination of the individual to the whole by identifying the state as the arbiter of the social good. Negative liberty represented the West, with its constitutional safeguards of individual rights; positive liberty the Soviet Union. Of course, the idea of freedom as the absence of restraint had deep roots in American history; but Berlin himself was alarmed by how readily his formulation was invoked not only against communism but to discredit the welfare state and anything that smacked of economic regulation. The absorption of his essay into the mainstream of liberal thought had the effect of marginalizing a different understanding of "positive" freedom as active citizen engagement in democratic politics advanced around the same time by Hannah Arendt.[28]

With the USSR replacing Germany as freedom's antithesis, the vaguely socialistic freedom from want—central to the Four Freedoms of World War II—slipped into the background or took on a very different meaning. Whatever Moscow stood for was by definition the opposite of freedom—and not merely one-party rule, suppression of free expression, and the like, but public housing, universal health insurance, full employment, and other claims that required strong and persistent government intervention in the economy. If freedom had an economic definition, it was no longer economic autonomy (as in the nineteenth century), "industrial democracy" (a rallying cry of the Progressive era), or economic security for the average citizen guaranteed by the government (as Roosevelt had defined it), but "free enterprise" and consumer autonomy—the ability to choose from the cornucopia of goods produced by the modern American economy. A common material culture of abundance would provide the foundation for global integration—eventually including even the communist world—under American leadership. The cold war helped to secure the glorification of "free enterprise" as the most fundamental form of American freedom, an idea promoted by ubiquitous political rhetoric, advertising campaigns, school programs, and newspaper editorials. Since the Free World contained so many despotic governments (even South Africa was a member in good standing), official definitions of that geopolitical construct tended to feature anticommunism and market economics more than political liberty.[29]

Although in the late 1960s and 1970s, with the collapse of the postwar ideological consensus and a series of economic and political crises, the cold war rhetoric of freedom eased considerably, it was reinvigorated by Ronald Reagan. The Great Communicator effectively united into a coherent whole the elements of cold war freedom—negative liberty (that is, limited government), free enterprise, and anticommunism—all in the service of a renewed insistence on America's global mission. Consciously employing rhetoric that echoed back at least two centuries, Reagan proclaimed that "by some divine plan . . . a special kind of people—people who had a special love for freedom" had been chosen to settle the North American continent. This exceptional history imposed on the nation an exceptional responsibility: "we are the beacon of liberty and freedom to all the world."[30]

Today, at least in terms of political policy and discourse, Americans still live in the shadow of the Reagan revolution. "Freedom" continues to occupy as central a place as ever in our political vocabulary, but it has been largely appropriated by libertarians and conservatives of one kind or another, from advocates of unimpeded market economics to armed militia groups insisting that the right to bear arms is the centerpiece of American liberty. The dominant constellation of definitions seems to consist of a series of negations—of government, of social responsibility, of a common public culture, of restraints on individual self-definition and consumer choice. Once the rallying cry of the dispossessed, freedom is today commonly invoked by powerful economic institutions to justify many forms of authority, even as on the individual level it often seems to suggest the absence of authority altogether.[31]

As we enter the twenty-first century, the process of globalization itself seems to be reinforcing this prevailing understanding of freedom, at least among political leaders of both major parties and journalistic cheerleaders who equate globalization with the worldwide ascendancy of American commodities, institutions, and values. A series of presidential administrations, aided and abetted by most of the mass media, have redefined both American freedom and America's historic mission to promote it for all mankind to mean the creation of a single global free market in which capital, natural resources, and human labor are nothing more than factors of production in an endless quest for greater productivity and profit. Meanwhile, activities with broader social aims, many of them previously understood as expressions of freedom, are criticized as burdens on international competitiveness. The prevailing ideology of the global free market assumes that the economic life of all countries can and should be refashioned in the image of the United States—the latest version of the nation's self-definition as model of freedom for the entire world. "In so many ways," writes Thomas Friedman, "globalization is us." "Us" to Friedman means the "spread of free-market capitalism to every country in the world" and the Americanization of global culture. Of course, what Friedman fails to take into account is that "us" is itself a complex and contested concept. There has always been more than one definition of America and of American freedom, and today there is more than one American vision of what globalization should be.[32]

For what one student of the subject calls "hyperglobalizers," globalization defines a new epoch in human history, in which a "global civilization" will supersede traditional cultures.[33] Having become irrelevant, the nation-state will wither away or at least surrender its economic functions. At the moment, however, rather than homogenizing the world, globalization seems to be creating all sorts of new cultural and political fissures and exacerbating old ones. The proliferation of social movements and sometimes violent conflicts based on ethnicity, religion, and local and regional cultures suggests that the arrival of a single global culture or consciousness is not yet at hand. But these developments do seem directly related to a decline in the traditional functions of the nation-state.

Politically speaking, the world is likely to remain divided into territorial states for many years to come. Nonetheless, globalization is raising profound questions about governance and accountability in the global economy and throwing into question traditional ideas about the relationship between political sovereignty, national identity, and freedom. Today the assets of some multinational corporations exceed the gross national products of the majority of the world's nations. Decisions that affect the day-to-day lives of millions of people are daily made by institutions—the World Bank, International Monetary Fund, and transnational corporations—that operate without a semblance of democratic accountability. By expanding "individual choice" and weakening the powers of governments, declares a recent account, globalization enhances freedom.[34] This definition, however, excludes from consideration such elements of freedom, also deeply rooted in the American experience, as self-government, economic autonomy, and social justice.

The relationship between globalization and freedom may be the most pressing political and social problem of the twenty-first century. Historically, rights have been derived from membership in a nation-state, and freedom often depends on the existence of political power to enforce it. "Without authorities, no rights exist." Perhaps, in the future, freedom will accompany human beings wherever they go, and a worldwide regime of "human rights" that knows no national boundaries will come into existence, complete with supranational institutions capable of enforcing these rights and international social movements bent on expanding freedom's boundaries. Thus far, however, economic globalization has occurred without a parallel internationalization of controlling democratic institutions.[35]

Like any other process rooted in history, globalization produces losers as well as winners. It creates and distributes wealth more rapidly than in the past, while simultaneously increasing inequality both within societies and in the world at large. The question for the twenty-first century is not whether globalization will continue, but globalization by whom, for whom, and under whose control. The fate of freedom is centrally involved in this question. It should not surprise us if the losers—those marginalized by globalization—adopt definitions of freedom rather different from those of the winners. It is not inevitable that globalization must take a single, neoliberal form or that economic openness requires a state's retreat from the social protection of its citizens.[36]

At the height of the cold war, in his brilliant and sardonic survey of American political thought, *The Liberal Tradition in America*, Louis Hartz observed that the internationalism of the postwar era seemed in some ways to go hand in hand with self-absorption and insularity. Despite its deepened worldwide involvement, the United States was becoming more isolated intellectually from other cultures. Prevailing ideas of freedom in the United States, Hartz noted, had become so rigid and narrow that Americans could no longer appreciate definitions of freedom, common in other countries, related to social justice and economic equality, "and hence are baffled by their use."[37]

Today Hartz's call for Americans to listen to the rest of the world, not simply lecture it about what liberty is, seems more relevant than ever. This may be difficult for a nation that has always considered itself a city upon a hill, a beacon to mankind. Yet American independence was proclaimed by those anxious to demonstrate "a decent respect to the opinions of mankind." In the global world of the twenty-first century, it is not the role of historians to instruct our fellow citizens on how they should think about freedom. But it is our task to insist that the discussion of freedom must transcend boundaries rather than reinforcing or reproducing them. In a global age, the forever-unfinished story of American freedom must become a conversation with the entire world, not a complacent monologue with ourselves.

FOUR

THE RUSSIANS WRITE
A NEW HISTORY

In 1990, I lived in Moscow for four months, teaching at Moscow State University as a Fulbright lecturer in American History. It was a remarkable historical moment. Mikhail Gorbachev was in power, pursuing his attempt to reform the Soviet system. Store shelves were nearly bare, but fear of political repression seemed to have vanished. My students and colleagues, ordinary citizens, and the press were completely open in expressing their dissatisfactions and their hopes for the future. In this national self-examination, history played a central role. I witnessed the forging of a new historical consciousness, which combined nostalgia for prerevolutionary days with a harshly critical assessment of the Soviet era. Views of American society and history were also being transformed. Once a pillar of the Soviet system, history had become a vehicle of widespread disenchantment.

Four years later, I returned to Moscow for an academic conference. The USSR was no more. Russia had been subjected to a dose of "shock therapy," and among the casualties were the utopian dreams I had encountered in 1990. A few Russians had become very rich while the mass of the population had been plunged into dire poverty. Interest in history had waned considerably, supplanted by the daily struggle for survival. Nor have living conditions improved much since.

Whatever the future holds, this essay, written on my return to the United States in 1990, recalls an extraordinary moment when Russians embarked on the task of reconceptualizing their nation's past.

•

Among Moscow's more fascinating exhibitions last spring was a small show at the Donskoy monastery about Solovki, an island in the icy seas off Archangel. Settled in the sixteenth century by Russian monks, who built a thriving community on the rocky, desolate terrain, Solovki became famous, or infamous, as a penal colony. The former monastery was first occupied by opponents of the czarist regime; then the whole island became a camp for Soviet political prisoners. Today Solovki is a tourist attraction.

Five years into the Gorbachev era, the Soviet Union finds itself completely rewriting its own history, and the Solovki exhibit, twice extended because of popular demand, illustrates the new thinking that has begun to reshape the Russian past. The exhibit explained, in loving detail, how the monks beat back the sea, dug irrigation canals, and achieved economic self-sufficiency. The island's use as a prison camp before 1917 was passed over with only the briefest mention, but the presentation of the 1920s and 1930s was unflinching—letters, photographs, and personal belongings of the artists, scientists, poets, and political dissenters who perished at Solovki. The show exemplified the current nostalgia among educated people for prerevolutionary days as well as the simultaneous reluctance to confront the unpleasant aspects of czarist society and the obsessive need to fill in the blank pages in the history of the Soviet era.

I had arrived in the Soviet Union at the beginning of February to teach nineteenth-century American history at Moscow State University. Early in my visit, a Soviet colleague remarked that the USSR is the land of the "unpredictable past," where historical judgments shift, often abruptly, in the prevailing political winds. Of course, history everywhere is political, in the sense that contemporary problems and values profoundly affect accounts of the past. But rarely has history been so malleable as in Gorbachev's Soviet Union. *Glasnost* (intellectual openness) provoked challenges to established verities in every corner of Soviet life. Simultaneously, under the slogan of *perestroika* (restructuring), Soviet authorities embarked on a series of reforms intended to transform the country's political and economic structure.

A new future requires a new past. To legitimize these far-reaching changes, the press and public officials painted the history of the Soviet era in the blackest hues, reclassifying every top leader between Lenin and Gorbachev as either criminal or incompetent. In high schools, textbooks on Soviet history have been scrapped, new ones have yet to appear, and last year final examinations in history were canceled altogether. The same struggle to keep up with new revelations about the past is evident in other venues where history is presented. When I visited Moscow's popular Museum of the Red Army, the rooms on the 1930s were closed. The exhibit, I was told, needed to be revamped in order to take into account newly released documents revealing how Stalin's purges of high-ranking officers contributed to the military disasters of 1941. One *glasnost*-inspired alteration had already taken place: a group portrait of the general staff in 1945 had been replaced by a painting of American and Soviet soldiers meeting at the Elbe.

More than the flood of new information, the collapse of established assumptions and previously unquestioned paradigms has produced an intellectual crisis. The demise of communist regimes in Eastern Europe and the crisis of the Soviet economy have thrown into question Marxist ideas that previously underpinned historical scholarship—that history is evolving in a predetermined direction, that capitalism is declining and socialism on the rise, that class struggle is the motive force of historical change.

"The old historical science has collapsed," remarked E. B. Chernyak, a leading "methodologist" (that is, an expert in what we would call theories of history) at Moscow's prestigious Institute of World History. But slowly and chaotically, a new history is emerging—a history interesting, provocative, and no less "political" than the old.

At Chernyak's institute, for example, several research projects are under way that reflect the "new thinking" of the Gorbachev era. One group has embarked on a study of the role of "great men" in historical change; another has adopted "civilization" as its key category for future study, replacing the Marxist "social and economic formation" and promising far greater attention to culture, religion, and other noneconomic aspects of historical development. Paralleling Gorbachev's desire to locate the USSR within a "common European home," scholarly projects are being launched in cooperation with historians from Western Europe, aimed at identifying the features Soviet history shares with that of the West. (Such "Eurocentrism" stands in striking contrast to the multicultural thrust of much current historical thinking in the United States and pointedly ignores the distinctiveness of the USSR's vast non-European population.)

The lexicon of scholarly discourse has itself changed. "Class" and "progress" are out, and during my four months in Moscow I never heard a mention of "imperialism." The concept of "revolution" is being rethought—turned on its head, really. Chernyak's view is that revolutions (like the French and Russian) that attempt to abolish the existing order entirely should be deemed less radical than "organic revolutions" (like the American), which build on existing institutions rather than destroying them. The reason? By reducing future social conflict, revolutions of the second sort create more favorable conditions for economic growth.

At the same time, the traditional Marxist distinction between "bourgeois" and socialist ideologies has given way to a search for "universal human values" (another Gorbachev byword, which seems oddly ahistorical, since it denies the significance of time and place in· establishing moral standards). These universal values have yet to be clearly defined, but thus far they bear a remarkable resemblance to features commonly associated with American life: respect for individual rights, constitutional limits on the powers of government, a high standard of living, even market relations and protection for private property (in the Soviet Union, usually referred to as "individual property" so as not to offend adherents of the "old thinking"). This love affair with America can lead to some remarkable conclusions. Since a socialist society is one that fully embodies "universal values," one scholar has proposed, the United States is actually more socialist than the Soviet Union.

Economic crisis has a way of inspiring a search for utopias abroad. In the 1930s, many American intellectuals found theirs in a Soviet Union apparently immune to the Great Depression's ravages. Russians, of course, have long viewed America as a country where all the qualities supposedly absent from their own society could be found. For decades, the press limited its reporting to America's ills: poverty, homelessness, racism, unemployment. Today criticism is out of fashion; America has become the land of liberty and prosperity of our own imagination. Writing in *Moscow News*, one historian declared that since Jefferson's Declaration of Independence, Americans have valued "freedom of the individual over everything else"—a statement that certainly would have surprised Jefferson's hundred slaves, to say nothing of the millions freed only by the Civil War.

As Soviet-American relations are transformed, a new account of the American experience is replacing the traditional interpretation. Nikolai Bolkovitinov, perhaps the USSR's leading scholar of American history, recently chided his colleagues for persistently misrepresenting the American Constitution. In his view, the Constitution, far from reflecting the outlook of the eighteenth-century bourgeoisie, as previous Soviet scholars would have it, embodied "universal human ideals," especially the concept of a "law-based state."

Given their country's history, it is not difficult to understand the appeal of a "law-based state," and one with fully stocked supermarkets to boot. But the new view of the United States is as one-dimensional as the one it is supplanting. Americans in Moscow today often find themselves reminding Soviet friends that our history has its own complement of mistakes and crimes, and that our present is not universally rosy.

At Bolkovitinov's invitation, I delivered a talk at the Institute of World History on blacks and the American Constitution. I discussed how the founding fathers had written protections for slavery, such as the obligation to return fugitives, into the document; how even free blacks had enjoyed few legal rights before the Civil War; and how it had taken almost a century for the promise of emancipation and Reconstruction to begin to be fulfilled.

Nothing I said would have seemed particularly controversial to American historians. But my talk was not, shall we say, greeted with enthusiasm. Listeners praised my research but seemed puzzled by my "oppositional" stance. One historian commented that although he did not agree with my interpretation, it was good for Soviet scholars to hear such views—as if my "take" on the subject were hopelessly eccentric. Another remarked that my rather bleak account of the economic condition of black America in the 1980s seemed at odds with the current Soviet interpretation of the Reagan years, which sees the lot of all Americans, including blacks, as improving markedly. I met a harsher reaction when I delivered the same lecture in Tbilisi, Georgia: a scholar of American history there chided me for leaving out the "fact" that much of our racial problem is caused by black women who "have six or seven children and expect white taxpayers to support them."

The same disenchantment with the previous orthodoxy and longing for a new past was evident among my students. In my first lecture, I remarked that the semester's themes held particular relevance for today's Soviet Union—the rise of the market, the causes of secession, and the process of radical reconstruction. (With luck, I added, the USSR could go nineteenth-century America one better and avoid a civil war.) In the very week when I lectured on the American secession crisis, Lithuania declared its independence. Gorbachev's response, I pointed out, was not unlike Lincoln's: a union, no matter how constructed, could not be dismantled without the consent of all its members.

To my surprise, nearly all my thirty-odd students supported Lithuania's right to leave the Soviet Union. Indeed, they viewed with remarkable equanimity the very real possibility of their country's dismemberment, especially if this could be accomplished without bloodshed. Nor did they express regret about the recent "loss" of Eastern Europe and the evident decline of the USSR's status as a great power. One student said that Gorbachev should take a lesson from Russia's policy after its defeat in the Crimean War, which revealed the country's profound social and economic backwardness: the USSR should retire from the world scene for a generation and put its own house in order.

Predictably, my students read American history through the prism of their own desires. On their final exams, for instance, nearly all professed admiration for Abraham Lincoln, whom they saw as a pragmatist guided solely by "common sense." Their nonideological Lincoln, who lacked deeply held political and moral convictions, would be unrecognizable to most American historians. The construct of a generation soured on ideology, he embodied their yearning for intellectual and political moderation after nearly a century of war and social upheaval.

As for their own history, my students shared the current obsession with locating missed opportunities and roads not taken in the Soviet past. Lately, the focus of this search has shifted backward. Three years ago, Lenin's New Economic Policy (NEP) of the early 1920s was praised as a more viable economic program than the system of centralized planning and control instituted by Stalin. There was widespread interest in Nikolai Bukharin, Lenin's colleague and an opponent of Stalin's policy of collectivization, who envisioned a more humane path to socialism. And long-proscribed avant-garde painters like Kazimir Malevich and Alexandra Exter received major exhibitions. A sharp line was drawn between Lenin's rule and Stalin's later tyranny.

Today, while Lenin is still widely revered as a kind of George Washington figure, the line between the 1920s and 1930s is gradually eroding. One day, walking with a graduate student near the university, I saw a poster for an exhibition of Liubov Popova, a cubist-turned-constructivist painter of the early revolutionary period. When I expressed admiration for her work, my companion launched into a tirade against Popova's entire modernist generation. Not only did they support the revolution, but their avant-garde art repudiated the old Russian culture of czarist days. That so many of these artists were silenced in the 1930s or died in Stalin's purges apparently made no difference.

As for Bukharin, three years ago, a colleague told me, a biography of him by American scholar Stephen F. Cohen was "the most popular book in Moscow." Today, he went on, no one cares about Bukharin or for that matter the NEP. The hero of the moment is Peter Stolypin, prime minister from 1906 until his assassination in 1911, who oversaw the brutal repression of the democratic movement of 1905, but then instituted a reform program that included peasant proprietorship and equality before the law.

The "Stolypin alternative," it is now said, might have "saved" Russia from revolution. One student insisted that czarist society was well on the way to transforming itself peacefully from an economically backward autocracy into a modern, democratic, capitalist society, when its progress was suddenly and inexplicably aborted by the Bolshevik Revolution. Without 1917, he continued, devising an implausible imaginary history for his country, the Russian monarchy would have tranquilly surrendered its power and assumed a purely symbolic role, as in today's England.

Even accomplishments of which all Soviets can be justly proud, such as the defeat of the Nazis in World War II, evoked little enthusiasm from my students. One of the USSR's most popular holidays is May 9, the anniversary of German surrender in 1945. This is when the parade of military hardware, which Americans erroneously associate with May Day, takes place, and when groups of veterans gather informally to sing, dance, and remember.

May 9 was a beautiful spring day this year, and I took my two-year-old daughter to Gorky Park and the square outside the Bolshoi Theater to see the veterans' gatherings. I found the experience affecting and somewhat sad. To my surprise, no young people took part in the celebrations. When I asked a student about this, he remarked, "My generation has no interest in May 9."

The rethinking of history, I realized, has opened a deep fissure between the generations. Filtered through memory, history gives meaning to people's experiences. For millions of older citizens, the struggles—at fearsome cost—to wrest a backward country into modernity and repel the Nazi invaders remain the central events of their lives. The bright light now illuminating the dark corners of Soviet history, they sense, is casting other parts—their parts—into shadow. They too crave a new past, but one that encompasses successes as well as failures, the sacrifices of idealistic men and women as well as monstrous crimes. They deeply resent having their ideals, struggles, and accomplishments forgotten or, worse still, dismissed by the media and younger generation as pointless. "I feel my life has been wasted," one lifelong communist remarked to me.

This older generation does not share the nostalgia for czarist days now fashionable among critics of the existing order. But at Moscow State, many students (themselves mostly from privileged families) lavished praise on the high standard of prerevolutionary culture and the excellence of elite prerevolutionary education, lamenting the downward "leveling" of both in the Soviet period. At the same time, they managed to overlook the most glaring weaknesses of czarist society—widespread illiteracy, social inequity, economic backwardness, and political bankruptcy. Indeed, this spring portraits of Nicholas II and his family were quickly sold out at the main university building. (A student managed to locate one for our going-away present.)

Such nostalgia is an enemy of true historical understanding, since it reifies portions of the past while ignoring others. But as a wholesale rejection of the present, nostalgia can serve as a powerful mode of protest. In eighteenth-century England, the idea of the "Norman Yoke"—that Anglo-Saxon England was democratic and egalitarian until William the Conqueror in 1066 imposed an aristocratic tyranny—helped inspire the movement for political reform and social justice. Today this kind of radical nostalgia is especially powerful in the Soviet Union's restive republics.

During my stay, I managed to visit Tallinn and Tbilisi, capitals, respectively, of Estonia and Georgia. A medieval trading port on the Baltic, Tallinn enjoys a prosperity Muscovites can only envy (and indeed, the city swarms with Russians who come to shop for the jewelry, food, and clothing that are hard to find elsewhere in the USSR). Nationalism is flourishing, complete with its own version of history. Time and again I heard the period between the two world wars—when Estonia, Latvia, and Lithuania enjoyed independence—referred to as a golden age. (The authoritarianism and pro-German sentiment of the independent Baltic states are forgotten.)

Partly because Soviet troops in 1989 killed some twenty pro-independence demonstrators in Tbilisi, the rethinking of history is even more sweeping there than in Estonia. Visible symbols of Soviet rule have all but disappeared. At the Georgia State Museum, which traces the region's history from the days of the Stone Age, the section covering the period after 1921 was closed, as if the last seven decades could somehow be erased. With one exception, every statue of Lenin in Tbilisi has been pulled down. The most popular historical shrine is now a huge cross in front of the city hall, commemorating those killed a year ago.

As in Estonia, I heard numerous remarks about how Georgia's citizens, when independent, had enjoyed universal peace and prosperity. Not being an expert on the republic's past, I was surprised to learn that Georgia, for centuries a part of the czarist empire, had enjoyed exactly four years of independence—from 1917 to 1921.

"A society cannot live or develop normally," said Yuri Afanasyev, "without knowing where it came from and what it is." Sometimes, as in Stalin's Soviet Union or the early-twentieth-century United States (where historians rewrote the American past to justify the denial of blacks' rights as citizens), history serves mainly to rationalize the status quo. History can degenerate into nostalgia for an imaginary golden age, or inspire a utopian quest to erase the past altogether. And it can force people to think differently about their society by bringing to light unpleasant truths. In today's Soviet Union, it is playing all these roles and more. It is easier, of course, to dismantle an old vision than to assemble a new one. But if historians succeed in providing this troubled country with a common sense of its past, they will have done as much as legions of radicals, secessionists, and populists to project the Soviet Union into a new future.

FIVE

"WE MUST FORGET THE PAST": HISTORY IN THE NEW SOUTH AFRICA

In the summer of 1994, I was invited to speak at a historical conference in South Africa. Only a few weeks earlier, in the first democratic election in the nation's history, Nelson Mandela had been elected president, ending centuries of white minority rule. As in the Soviet Union a few years earlier, hopes for a radical transformation of people's lives abounded. And, as in that earlier experience, a history created to reinforce the old regime was being completely rethought, often in surprising ways and not without sometimes bitter debate. The essay that follows was written on my return to the United States.

In the summer of 1999, I returned to South Africa. The transition from apartheid to democracy was still under way, its ultimate outcome still uncertain. History remained a national preoccupation. The prison on Robben Island where Mandela and other leaders of the African National Congress were long held was now a major tourist attraction (with former inmates and Mandela's ex-jailer among the guides). District Six,

mentioned at the outset of the essay below, was still a wasteland, but the government had pledged to rebuild it for descendants of those evicted half a century ago. At its center now
stood a museum containing photographs and other mementos
that kept alive the memory of a thriving neighborhood destroyed by apartheid.

South Africa in 1999 was riveted by testimony before the
Truth and Reconciliation Commission, which offered amnesty
to government officials and anti-apartheid fighters who candidly
acknowledged past crimes. The commission embodied the new
government's conviction that national self-understanding is
more important than punishment, and that the uncompromis-
ing exposure of historical evils is a prerequisite to national
reconciliation.

•

R inged by mountains that reach almost to the Atlantic
shore, Cape Town, South Africa, has a majestic setting that residents like to compare with San Francisco's. To me, however, Cape Town brings to mind Los
Angeles. In both cities, natural environments of extraordinary
beauty heighten one's awareness of the destructive handiwork
of man. In Los Angeles, urban sprawl has covered a vast region
with tract housing and freeways and saturated the air with
smog. In Cape Town, the physical separation of peoples and
vast differences of power and wealth are the living legacy of
apartheid. Near the city center stands District Six, once a thriving community of Cape Coloureds (people of mixed racial
ancestry), now a desolate wasteland dotted by churches, the

only buildings left standing when the government decreed twenty years ago that nonwhites could no longer live in central Cape Town.

Today, in fact, there exist several Cape Towns, separate and extremely unequal—the city center and adjacent beach communities inhabited by whites; a nearby belt of Coloured housing; an older and poorer community of black Africans; and a vast expanse of squatter shacks that stretch as far as the eye can see from the city's outskirts. Here live nearly one million people, most of whom lack electricity and running water. Cape Town's physical geography reflects how heavily the burden of history weighs on this land even as it moves into a new era.

As in many of the world's old port cities, Cape Town's waterfront has recently found a new lease on life as a site of commercial development. From San Francisco to Cardiff, seaports experiencing commercial decline have redefined their proximity to the sea as a leisure and tourist attraction. In one respect, however, Cape Town's waterfront is unique, for the visitor encounters not only a sanitized environment of upscale shops and hotels but a series of thirty-two historical panels offering a startlingly revisionist account of the port's history. Produced by historians at the University of Cape Town and installed only a few months ago by the waterfront company that governs the development, the text and visual images trace the history of the port's racially diverse working population, including slave and indentured labor in the shipping and construction industries. One panel directs the visitor's attention to nearby Robben Island, "one of the world's most notorious political prisons," where Nelson Mandela spent years "for resisting apartheid."

Interestingly, the only panel that produced sustained objections from the Waterfront Company was one observing how the fishing industry has changed over time from an enterprise of small operators to a monopoly. Thought to cast contemporary business in an unflattering light, this has been removed for rewording. But as for the rest, they reflect the fact that the "new history" has commercial appeal. Frankly acknowledging the troubled past makes the area seem up to date, in tune with the spirit of post-apartheid South Africa.

The waterfront is not the only place in Cape Town where traditional presentations of history are being reconsidered and new ones developed. Under the old regime, the government made strenuous efforts to demonstrate that Africans had no history. In 1964, Cape Town's South African Museum, founded in 1825 and the oldest museum in sub-Saharan Africa, was divided in two. A new Cultural History Museum traced the region's history from the time of its discovery by Europeans, while the South African Museum was left to showcase the country's natural history and African anthropology. Black Africans, as curator Patricia Davidson notes, were removed from history and "put in with the animals."

If the ideology of apartheid insisted upon eliminating Africans from history, the new South Africa must obviously put them back in. But this is easier said than done. Despite the South African Museum's dramatic exhibits of whales, fossils, and the like, its most popular presentation, to the chagrin of forward-looking curators, remains a diorama of primitive Bushmen in the African wild. Like *Coloured* and *African* (the word for unmixed descendants of the indigenous population), *Bushman* is a political concept, not a scientific one. Invented by white colonizers, it has been applied to diverse peoples who lived by hunting and gathering but who did not see themselves as belonging to the same population.

Should the Bushman diorama be removed? Should it survive as an artifact of how Africans used to be conceptualized? As a temporary compromise, the museum has decided to retain the diorama, while amending, historicizing, and "problematizing" it. Until recently the diorama, reminiscent of old issues of *National Geographic,* presented a "Bushwoman" reclining unclothed in front of a tent. Although women in traditional African societies sometimes went bare-breasted, there is no evidence whatever that they lay about stark naked, and Davidson has had the figure draped with a cloth. In addition, new labels question the diorama's implicit assumptions that traditional culture is permanent and unchanging and that Africans are native only to rural areas. (In fact, as one new label discloses, the Bushman life casts, made in 1911, were actually of people living in settlements near Cape Town.) Now a photograph of urban black life is juxtaposed to the diorama, and alongside the traditional cloth, tools, and sculpture are new cases with items made by Africans today, such as T-shirts, union buttons, and beaded dolls depicting policemen and other figures from modern city life. Africans, the museum wants visitors to understand, have never resided outside of history in an "unchanging past."

Other Cape Town institutions have also moved to revise their presentation of history, to "Africanize" themselves, in a term much heard in today's South Africa. The Cape Town Art Museum has placed exhibitions of African art alongside its traditional European collections. The Castle, long a military headquarters, recently hosted an exhibit on the city's Muslim community. Even the Cultural History Museum, while retaining a definite colonial feel, has introduced a few items relating to the indigenous population amid the rooms portraying British and Dutch explorers and colonial officials, with their clothing, furniture, ceramics, and weaponry. But upstairs the museum's breathless race through the human past, beginning with ancient Egypt, Greece, Rome, and China, still leaves out Africa south of the Sahara, as if this formed no part of the history of civilization.

Even fewer have been the changes at the Village Museum in Stellenbosch, an Afrikaner town at the center of the Western Cape's wine district, where slavery flourished into the nineteenth century. The museum's four nicely restored houses, ranging from a seventeenth-century farm dwelling to an upper-class Victorian home, contain no mention of the slaves, servants, and black laborers who built these homes; nor are slave quarters included in the restorations. The presentation of history still reinforces the Afrikaners' self-conception as a people who settled in an uninhabited wilderness and depended on no one but themselves for economic success.

I had come to South Africa for the first time in July 1994 to speak at a conference on the history of democracy. According to the newspapers, we live in an era of democratic renewal; since 1980, scores of countries in Europe, Latin America, and Africa have sloughed off dictatorships of one form or another and embraced the democratic ideal (or at least held elections). Yet in many cases, democracy has produced economic chaos, ethnic conflict, and a deep sense of disillusionment. Where it has existed far longer, democracy also seems to be in some sort of crisis. In the United States, only half the eligible population bothers to vote, political parties are moribund, and the people's elected representatives are widely held in contempt. In Britain, the government of Conservative Prime Minister John Major lacks any semblance of public support; much of the recent political leadership of Italy is in prison. South Africa, by contrast, had just experienced its first democratic elections, a deeply emotional experience for blacks and whites alike and a time of hope for the majority of its population.

The conference was held at the University of the Witwatersrand in Johannesburg and sponsored by History Workshop, a loosely organized group of scholars who over the past twenty years have produced some of the world's finest historical scholarship. Inspired in part by British and American neo-Marxist social history, scholars associated with History Workshop have rewritten South African history to emphasize the experience of black laborers in rural areas and in urban mines and industries. Their work shows how the South African state systematically destroyed a thriving African peasantry and how apartheid was not simply a form of racial separation but a means of creating a dispossessed, closely controlled labor force for white-owned enterprises. Like "history from below" in other countries, this new South African history has given voice to those excluded from traditional accounts, often through oral histories that allow ordinary people to relate their lives and express their aspirations. Even more than elsewhere, the new history has been politically engaged, written to expose the bases of racial and class oppression in South Africa as a contribution to the struggle against apartheid. I assumed that with apartheid dead and Nelson Mandela newly inaugurated as South Africa's president, historians would be in a festive mood. This did not, to my surprise, prove to be the case.

The conference reinforced my impression of the high quality of South African historical writing. The hundred-odd papers

ranged from studies of popular movements in particular locali-
ties and life histories of participants in the struggle against
apartheid, to sweeping evaluations of international trends
on issues like agrarian reform and state formation. Discussions
were serious and, to use a now-archaic term, comradely. Perhaps understandably, most papers concentrated on the recent
past, and the most animated debates concerned the recent elections and the future. One participant apologized for giving a
paper that went back to the 1920s, and as for the nineteenth
century, it was almost never mentioned.

Rather than celebration, the prevailing mood was one of
foreboding, not only about South Africa's future but also about
the future of history itself. "History," one participant jested,
"is fast replacing economics as the dismal science." A host of
specters seemed to be haunting the conference, first among
them a way of understanding modern world politics known to
political scientists as "transition theory." This argues, in brief,
that the transition from authoritarian government to democracy is best accomplished not by revolutionary upheaval but by
negotiations between reformers in the ruling regime and mod-
erates among the opposition. Fifty years ago, the American historian Carl Becker observed that democracy functions best
when political issues center on superficial problems rather than
deep social divisions. Transition theory builds on this idea,
insisting that for a democratic transition to be successful, major
social questions (such as the redistribution of wealth) must
be kept off the political agenda. The resulting system is often
called "thin" or "low density" democracy: the previously disenfranchised majority is empowered, but the old elite retains considerable authority, and the structure of society remains largely
unchanged.

Devised in the 1980s to explain the emergence of democratic political systems in South America and Eastern Europe, transition theory is both descriptive and prescriptive, an account of change in deeply fractured societies and an argument in favor of a political democracy that coexists quite comfortably with vast inequalities of wealth and power. At the History Workshop conference, it came in for well-deserved criticism as a formula for things to change so that they may remain the same. But beneath these discussions lay the suspicion that transition theory offered a not-implausible account of what has actually taken place in South Africa. Like two exhausted swimmers forced to cling to each other to avoid drowning (to paraphrase a passage from *Macbeth*), the African National Congress (ANC) and Afrikaner state had, by the late 1980s, become dependent on each other. Popular resistance had made South Africa ungovernable, but the ANC and allied groups lacked the power to overturn the old order. Meanwhile South Africa had become an international pariah, and it was clear that some sort of change was inevitable. This occurred through prolonged, mostly secret negotiations, which produced elections whose results were agreed upon in advance by the major parties and a "government of national unity" in which representatives of the apartheid state retain considerable power, civil servants keep their jobs, and the police and armed forces remain pretty much unchanged. Compared to the dream of liberation that animated anti-apartheid activists in the 1980s, the transition that actually occurred seems tame and the results ambiguous and disorienting. "The ANC has the government," one historian remarked to me, "but the Afrikaner still has the state." Another remarked even more cynically, "We live under black majority white rule."

The new constitution reflects another series of compromises between old and new. In affirming the right of all South Africans to equal rights and opportunities regardless of race, gender, sexual orientation, or other attributes, the constitution is among the most democratic in the world. These provisions, however, stand in uneasy juxtaposition to others recognizing the traditional powers of African chiefs and the authority of customary tribal law, which has historically operated in blatantly discriminatory ways, especially toward women. Yet this was the price of winning the support of tribal authorities for the negotiated transition.

Democracy has replaced *liberation* as the key word in the language of politics, an odd situation, in a way, in a country that lacks a deeply rooted democratic tradition. Every day brings conversions to the virtues of multiracial democracy by former proponents of apartheid. ("The road to Damascus is in gridlock," one conference participant remarked.) But democracy means very different things to different South Africans. It is the name given by blacks to their aspirations for better lives—jobs, housing, education, and the opportunities denied them under the old regime—and by whites to their hope of retaining their social privileges (now defended in the name not of racial superiority but of minority rights, pluralistic politics, and the sanctity of private property).

Two centuries ago, America's founding fathers agonized over the relationship between democracy and private property. Would not the poor, James Madison asked at the Constitutional Convention, use the suffrage to despoil the rich? Yet history has demonstrated that, for better or worse, universal suffrage can easily coexist not only with private property as an institution but with a highly unequal distribution of wealth. No one expects the accumulated wealth of white South Africa simply to be redistributed among the blacks (despite white fears before the elections that this was precisely what blacks had in mind). Blacks do assume, however, that the advent of democracy will bring tangible benefits. During my visit, black workers initiated a wave of strikes for wage increases and an easing of the country's highly authoritarian work rules. Meanwhile squatters unwilling to wait for a promised program of land distribution occupied municipal land. The business community views such actions as highly destabilizing and is pressuring the government to remain "neutral" in labor disputes (something the old regime never was) in order to maintain the proper climate for foreign investment.

Also contributing to the mood of disquiet was the sense that a democratic South Africa is taking its place on the world stage at precisely the moment when basic economic decisions are made by multinational corporations and institutions like the World Bank and International Monetary Fund, not the nation-state. Speaker after speaker expressed disappointment with the fruits of independence in Africa. One of the most entertaining, and most disturbing, presenters was Owen Sichone of the University of the Witwatersrand, who satirized the entire idea of national independence in Africa as a form of "carnivalesque" theater offering the illusion of sovereignty in a world where outsiders make the fundamental decisions. The utopian dreams decolonization inspired seem to have vanished.

In many ways, of course, South Africa's social and economic situation is far better than that of other African states. The economy is much more diversified, and wages, although low by American standards, are far higher than elsewhere on the continent—the result of the militant trade union activity of the past twenty years. The wage gap between South African blacks and workers in neighboring African states, one economist told me, is about the same as between the United States and Mexico. The resulting influx of African immigrants into the country has provoked a backlash among those who feel their jobs are threatened. One resident of Soweto, speaking on a radio call-in show, recently proposed reestablishing the hated pass system to keep out cheap foreign labor.

South Africa, in fact, is a combination of a modern Western nation and a poor Third World country. It can build an atomic bomb and put a satellite into orbit, but a majority of its economically active population is functionally illiterate, and 60 percent of its homes lack electricity and indoor plumbing. Along with Brazil, South Africa has the most unequal distribution of income in the world. Vast numbers of Africans live in squalid shacks on the outskirts of South African cities or in impoverished rural "homelands." The ANC won the election of April 1994 on a program of bringing the rights of "social citizenship"—free health care, adequate housing, unemployment insurance, universal public education—to the black majority that has been systematically excluded from the benefits of South Africa's economic growth. These promises were widely publicized; three months after the election, the ANC's *Reconstruction and Development Program* was still the number one paperback best-seller. But since his election, Mandela has gone to great lengths to assure whites that uplifting the black poor does not mean lowering the white standard of living and to caution his black constituency that change will be gradual, not immediate. Hovering over Mandela is the threat of capital flight, currency collapse, and lack of outside investment if his government threatens vested economic interests.

Where does hope lie of resisting or reversing these disturb-ing trends? As an alternative to the "thin democracy" of deci-sions imposed from above, some papers invoked the grassroots democracy embodied in "civil society"—a catchall term used to describe "private" institutions that lie outside the purview of the state's public power. A mobilized civil society, including unions, civic associations in black townships, church groups, and student organizations helped bring down the apartheid regime. These movements, a number of papers vividly demon-strated, drew on long-established social networks, kinship ties, and other relationships that were not in themselves "political" to galvanize resistance.

The invocation of civil society as a source of grassroots democracy and an alternative to governmental domination of everyday life has become a staple of contemporary political discourse, a natural reaction to the history of state-centered authoritarianism in South Africa and other parts of the world. Civil society, however, is not simply an alternative source of democratic values; as some commentators pointed out, it is also the site of some extremely undemocratic practices. Traditional communities are highly authoritarian and patriarchal, qualities strongly reinforced by the apartheid state, which enhanced the local power of chiefs and bolstered the authority of employers over labor and husbands over their wives. The public-private dichotomy itself may be highly misleading, since public power often shapes the context within which private relationships exist. American history clearly demonstrates the critical role of a powerful national government in democratizing civil soci-ety—for example, in combating racial inequality.

If anything seems to characterize African civil society, it is the power of tribal and ethnic loyalties, even in the face of the past generation's strenuous efforts to build a nation. "Without doubt," declared a participant who spoke on Kenya, "ethnicity has emerged as the dominant factor in politics." But this issue was rarely mentioned by those who talked about South Africa. Given the frightening realities of Bosnia and, nearer home, Rwanda, one can well appreciate the scholar's embrace of the ANC's avowed policy of nonracialism.

Although identification with the national state may be far stronger in South Africa than in other African nations at the time of their independence, ethnicity remains a threat to the new political order, and, indeed, to the nation's integrity itself. Already, South Africa's neighbors—Swaziland, Lesotho, Botswana—have laid claim to parts of the country that were erroneously (they claim) separated from theirs when imperial powers drew Africa's borders. Their premise that each ethnic group deserves its own nation-state was, in a warped way, an intellectual underpinning of apartheid, reinforcing the idea that blacks were citizens of "independent" homelands rather than of South Africa itself. In its campaign of "ethnicity building," the apartheid state was a master of what historians call "the invention of tradition," and for this reason the politics of ethnic identity arouses great hostility in ANC circles. But ethnic identity may have more resonance at the local level than one would like to believe. Once "invented," politically produced tribal loyalties have a way of taking on a life of their own.

The new South Africa has gone to enormous lengths to make all citizens, of whatever racial or ethnic identity, feel at home. The country now has eleven "official" languages, creating nightmares for civil servants and presenting intractable difficulties for schools, where the proper language of instruction is a heated point of debate. (English, already all-pervasive on television and in popular culture, seems destined eventually to become South Africa's de facto lingua franca). Authorities look to historians, among others, to contribute to a "nationalization of the consciousness." Elsewhere in Africa, enormous demands have been placed on historians to write the kind of nationalist Whiggish history that for so long dominated European scholarship, in which the nation-state was not only the focus of analysis but the preordained end of historical development. The historian's task was to create an intellectually plausible lineage for the nation's triumph.

Many African historians have readily accepted this role. Kenyan historiography, one scholar demonstrated, is dominated by the achievement of national independence; the Mau Mau movement is the privileged subject, while traditional phenomena that seem to have little to do with nationalism, like magic, popular mythologies, and ethnic rivalries, are downplayed or ignored. Many South African historians, without quite intending to do so, are now producing an ANC-centered history, constructing narratives that highlight the (perhaps exceptional) multiethnic and multiracial cooperation of the 1980s that overthrew apartheid. Yet the popular mobilizations of the past two decades owed much to African nationalism and the black consciousness movement, subjects ignored by nearly all the speakers. This is not to deny the power in today's South Africa of the ANC's nonracialism (a refreshing exception to the worldwide upsurge of nationalisms based on religion, ethnicity, language, and the like) but simply to say that this is a fairly recent development rather than a long-standing indigenous political tradition.

The dilemma of South African popular history today is that historians may not produce the history the "people" are looking for. Many black students imagine precolonial Africa as an egalitarian, democratic idyll; whites often envision it as a barren landscape peopled by barbarians. When it is written, a new history will not only have to avoid the temptation of succumbing to these myths but must be broad enough to encompass the full diversity of this society. (Rarely or never mentioned at the History Workshop conference were the history of Asian, Indian, and, most surprisingly perhaps, Afrikaner South Africans.)

And where will this new history be produced? Uneasiness over political and economic trends has combined with disquiet about the future of the university. Like everything else, South African higher education was shaped and misshaped by apartheid. Until thirty-five years ago, the law did not bar Africans, Coloureds, or Indians from attending college with whites, but lack of funds and the sorry state of nonwhite primary education ensured that their numbers would be small. Then, in 1959, the government ordered universities to be segregated by race and soon embarked on the construction of institutions for nonwhite students. The result was a crazy-quilt pattern in which white universities (most of which conducted classes in English, but some in Afrikaans) existed alongside a handful of separate and highly unequal institutions for blacks, Coloureds, or Indians. (The "color" of these latter universities referred to the students, not the faculty, who until the mid-1980s were primarily white graduates of conservative Afrikaans universities.) South African higher education also includes fifteen institutes of technology (really vocational training centers), called technikons, that now account for one-quarter of the country's 400,000 advanced students.

University apartheid crumbled in the late 1980s, and many white institutions began admitting nonwhite students, a process that has accelerated greatly in the past two years. The University of the Witwatersrand, the country's leading research institution, is now about one-fourth black, and at Cape Town, Africans make up half the entering class. The "historically Coloured" University of the Western Cape, built in the 1960s, has undergone a similar transformation. And African enrollment at the technikons has also risen rapidly in recent years. In all these institutions (even the technikons), black students overwhelmingly enter the humanities and social sciences, because math preparation in black schools has been virtually nonexistent. In terms of education, one economist told me, "our situation is completely deplorable": of every ten thousand African students in primary or secondary school, he went on, only one graduates able to do college-level math work. As a popular saying has it, Bantu education (the old term for African schools) was no education at all.

South African universities are today in turmoil as they face an uncertain future. Historically white and Coloured universities have made a major effort to attract black students, offering them financial support and, where necessary, remedial training. The recruitment of black faculty is also proceeding, albeit much more slowly. But in an echo of U.S. struggles of the 1960s and contemporary debates over affirmative action, black student groups are demanding the full "Africanization" of the universities, specifically that the student body and faculty reflect the proportion of blacks in the overall population (over 80 percent). At the same time, black universities, starved for money under the old regime, are demanding that traditional funding formulas be radically revised. Meanwhile the government, urged on by the World Bank, is considering a wholesale shift of educational resources to the primary level and into technical training, on the grounds that upgrading the largely illiterate and unskilled labor force is the key to economic development and social progress. Since 1985, half of South Africa's university degrees have been in the humanities and social sciences. This is a luxury that the government now says the country can no longer afford.

When combined with the stark reality that faculty salaries and university budgets have for years lagged behind inflation, and the knowledge that lack of resources has led to a collapse of higher education in other African countries, these developments have produced a deep sense of disquiet among academics at elite, research-oriented universities. Under apartheid, some white historians were jailed, deported, or prevented from publishing; they certainly suffered for their opposition to the regime. Compared with the majority of the population, however, all academics occupy positions of privilege in South Africa. As became obvious at the conference, teachers at nonwhite institutions see their counterparts at the elite universities, whatever their political stance, as part of the establishment. Indeed, very few scholars from the traditionally nonwhite universities even took part in the gathering, in part because these institutions lack facilities for research, and in part because the new history has not been effectively disseminated at African institutions of higher learning. The conference was one of the most racially integrated academic gatherings in South African history. But nearly all the black participants came from the United States (including black Americans and Africans in exile), from elsewhere in Africa, or from traditionally white South African institutions. Moreover, demands for admitting more Africans to the University of the Witwatersrand and Cape Town provoke fears of a future of academic mediocrity, the end of the research-oriented university as scholars have known it. Having once taught at New York's City College, I was repeatedly asked about (somewhat exaggerated) reports of the collapse of educational standards that followed the introduction of open admissions there in the early 1970s. Some academics seem to yearn for their own version of a transition guided by elites in which old structures remain largely intact.

Ultimately, the most troublesome question that hung over the Johannesburg conference concerned the role of history itself—its study, teaching, and social impact—in the new South Africa. To some extent, social history's problems are universal. In a world in which work, for many people, is no longer the most profound source of identity and socialism has collapsed both as a political system and as an intellectual ideal, social history has been searching for new paradigms. In South Africa, as elsewhere, some scholars have turned to the writings of structuralist theorists like Michel Foucault (cited, by my count, in more footnotes than Karl Marx) and his insistence that power must be studied not only in its formal legal dimension and in its economic sources and manifestations but in how it is diffused throughout society and embodied in local institutions as diverse as schools, churches, and families. Other historians find in the writing of "postcolonial" theorists like Edward Said a telling critique of how scholars from dominant nations have historically "constructed" Third World peoples as primitive, exotic "others" in order to justify imperial domination. (Cape Town's Bushman diorama offers a good example.)

Drawing on Foucault, Said, and others, sociologist Winston Leroke directly challenged South Africa's white social researchers, claiming that while combating apartheid they have been blind to the power relations inherent in their own work. White researchers constructing the "oral histories" of illiterate Africans, said Leroke, inadvertently reproduce the inequalities of the larger society. The African speaks, and the white social researcher (himself "illiterate" in the African language) receives the information in translation via an African research assistant and then organizes the knowledge. Africans, Leroke concluded, need to be able to speak for themselves.

Few scholars rose to Leroke's challenge to rethink the implications of the practice of history, in part because of the ambiguity of his argument itself. Was Leroke saying that only Africans can write about other Africans (and only whites about whites)? Would not similar power relations exist between a university-educated African scholar and an illiterate African subject? Does not the postmodernist critique verge on anti-intellectualism, implying that no one can write about anyone else without inevitably constituting the subject of investigation as an "object"? When asked what scholars ought to do, Leroke commented, "Perhaps we should just write about ourselves." Whatever the problems of his analysis, however, Leroke did make clear that white scholars cannot simply think of themselves as "raceless" practitioners of empirical research untouched by the structures of power created and maintained by apartheid.

Even as South African historians grapple with the postmodernist question of the relationship between historical writing and political power, they face an entirely different challenge: the new government's avowed policy of national reconciliation. The most recent issue of the ANC's magazine, *Mayibuye*, with the words "Free at Last" emblazoned on the cover, contains an interview with President Mandela. To the historian, Mandela's most arresting statement came in response to a question about amnesty for crimes committed by the old security forces: "We must forget the past."

To some extent, I sympathize with Mandela's admonition. Vengeance, C.L.R. James once remarked, has no place in politics. The spirit of reconciliation does indeed run deep among South Africans. When London-based scholar Shula Marks entered the country for the conference and listed her profession on the entry form, the immigration official remarked, "We don't need historians anymore."

We can forget the past, but the past, most assuredly, will not forget us. The experience of dead generations, Karl Marx once wrote, "weighs like a nightmare on the brain of the living." Indeed, it is difficult to think of a country where the past bears more directly on the present than South Africa, so thoroughly was the social structure, physical environment, even the language shaped by apartheid. Throughout this century, the government of South Africa intervened more heavy-handedly, and with more singularity of purpose, to shape the entire social order than in nearly any other country. The privileges enjoyed by whites as well as some Coloureds and Indians, and the abject conditions under which millions of Africans are forced to live, are the living products of this history. It was government policy, from the Land Act of 1913 to later laws mandating the forcible removal of tens of thousands of Africans from Johannesburg, Cape Town, and other cities, that reserved the vast majority of arable land and urban homesites for whites. The new government has announced the ambitious goal of transferring public land to 600,000 black families over the next five years, and it has set up a commission to investigate claims for compensation by those evicted from land back to 1913. Yet ironically, one scholar at the History Workshop conference complained, in formulating its land policy the government has consulted economists, geographers, citizens' associations—but not historians. What to remember and what to forget are themselves political questions, points of conflict as South Africa moves into a new era. If history teaches anything, it is that freedom is not achieved in a day; nor, once achieved, does it necessarily last forever. The price of maintaining freedom, as an Irish judge commented two centuries ago, is "eternal vigilance." And in that vigilance, historians have a vital role to play—reminding South Africans how they arrived at today's situation and of what remains to be done to make the dream of democracy and liberation not merely a political slogan but a living reality.

SIX

WHY IS THERE
NO SOCIALISM IN
THE UNITED STATES?

꧁꧂

In 1983, I was invited to take part in a conference exploring the failure of socialism in the United States, held at the Centre d'Etudes Nord-Américaines in Paris. Three years earlier, a Socialist-Communist coalition had elected François Mitterrand president of France, while Ronald Reagan had swept to an electoral victory in the United States. This stark political contrast reinvigorated the old debate about why European and American politics and class relations seemed so divergent. My paper reviewed the voluminous literature on American "exceptionalism," took issue with some of its underlying premises, and called for a more sophisticated understanding of the history of other countries with which the United States is often compared. Little did I imagine that the tentative suggestion with which the essay concludes would be soon be borne out by events across the globe, including the collapse of the Soviet Union, the disappearance of the Communist party of Italy, the repudiation by the British Labour party of the socialist elements in its party platform, and the rapid decline of socialism in the Third World. Today the question "Why is there no socialism in the United States?" appears rather arcane. But it does draw attention to the unexamined assumptions that still shape much American historical writing.

•

It is now nearly eighty years since the German sociologist Werner Sombart raised the question "Why is there no socialism in the United States?" In the ensuing decades, the problem has been a source of apparently endless debate among historians examining the distinctive qualities of the American experience, American radicals seeking an explanation for their political weakness, and Europeans alternately fascinated and repelled by the capitalist colossus to their west. Indeed, long before Sombart, the exceptional economic and political history of the United States commanded attention on both sides of the Atlantic.

Marx and Engels themselves occasionally sought to solve the riddle of America, the land where, as Marx once put it, capitalism had developed more "shamelessly" than in any other country. They could never quite decide, however, whether the unique qualities of nineteenth-century American life boded well or ill for the future development of socialism. Would the early achievement of political democracy prove an impediment to class consciousness in the United States or encourage it by making inequalities appear all the more illegitimate? Was the absence of a feudal tradition a barrier to the development of class-based ideologies, or did it make possible the early emergence of a modern socialist political culture? If America was, in so many ways, the most capitalist nation on earth, should it not also become the most socialist? Marx and Engels never answered such questions to their own satisfaction, and subsequent writers who have entered into the "why is there no socialism" quagmire have rarely been more successful.[1]

In the end, Marx and Engels remained optimistic about prospects for socialism in the United States. (Engels even advised the "backward" workers of Britain to learn from the example of the Knights of Labor.) Other observers, however, believed that the nature of American society precluded the emergence of political ideologies on the European model. In 1867, E. L. Godkin, the Irish-born editor of *The Nation*, sought to explain why, despite a wave of strikes in the United States, the "intense class feeling" so evident in Great Britain could not exist in America:

> There [in Europe] the workingman on a strike is not simply a laborer who wants more wages: he is a member of a distinct order in society, engaged in a sort of legal war with the other orders. . . . His employer is not simply a capitalist in whose profits he is seeking a larger share: he is the member of a hostile class, which . . . it is considered mean or traitorous for him to hope to enter. This feeling, we need hardly say, does not exist in America. The social line between the laborer and the capitalist here is very faintly drawn. Most successful employers of labor have begun by being laborers themselves; most laborers hope . . . to become employers. Moreover, there are . . . few barriers of habit, manners or tradition between the artisan and those for whom he works, so that he does not consider himself the member of an "order." Strikes, therefore, are in the United States more

a matter of business, and less a matter of sentiment, than in Europe. . . . Should the worse come to the worst [the American worker] has the prairies behind him, a fact which . . . diffuses through every workshop an independence of feeling, a confidence in the future, of which the European knows nothing. Besides this, the American working class are in the enjoyment of political power.[2]

I have quoted Godkin at some length, because the "why is there no socialism" debate has not advanced very far beyond the answers he proposed over a century ago. Godkin touched upon nearly all the elements from which modern responses to the question are generally forged: American ideology, social mobility, the nature of the union movement, the political structure. In this essay, I propose to examine the most recent trends in this seemingly timeless debate. The essay is not meant as a history of socialism in the United States, or as an exhaustive survey of the immense body of literature that now exists on the subject (since nearly every work on American radicalism and labor explicitly or implicitly proposes an answer to the question "Why is there no socialism?"). It will not examine expressions of American radicalism such as abolitionism and feminism, whose impact upon American life has been far more profound than socialism. I hope, however, to draw attention to the most recent contributions to this debate and to raise questions about both the adequacy of specific explanations and the underlying premises upon which the entire discussion appears to rest. It might well be worth raising at the outset the question whether the experience of socialism in the United States is, in reality, exceptional, or whether it represents an extreme example of the dilemma of socialism throughout Western society.

To some extent, the "Why is there no socialism?" debate remains inconclusive because the participants define socialism in diverse, sometimes contradictory ways. It is often unclear precisely what it is whose absence is to be explained. When Sombart wrote, in the period before World War I, there existed a reasonably unified body of socialist theory and political practice. But since the shattering of the international labor and socialist movements by World War I, the Russian Revolution, the rise of socialist and communist parties and indeed governments hostile to one another but both claiming the mantle of "socialism," and the emergence of new forms of socialism in the Third World, it is impossible to contend that "socialism" retains a coherent meaning. Socialism itself possesses a history, but too often contributors to the debate treat it as an ahistorical abstraction.

Nevertheless, by common consent, the extremely imprecise problem "Why is there no socialism in the United States?" has been reduced to a discrete set of questions. It does not mean "Why has the United States not become a socialist nation?" or even "Why is there no revolutionary labor or political movement?" Rather, the problem is generally defined as the absence in the United States of a large avowedly social democratic political party like the Labour party of Britain, the French Socialist party, and the Communist party of Italy. From the strength of such parties, moreover, American writers generally infer a mass socialist consciousness among the working classes of these countries. Thus, "Why is there no socialism?" really means "Why is the United States the only advanced capitalist nation whose political system lacks a social democratic presence and whose working class lacks socialist class consciousness?"

Posed this way, the question does seem to have a prima facie plausibility, although, as I will suggest, it may well rest on assumptions about western European politics and class relations that are out of date today and that may never have been fully accurate. One must, in other words, be wary of explanations for American exceptionalism that are based upon trends and phenomena equally evident in other countries. But this is only one of the pitfalls that characterize many analyses of the problem. Too often it is assumed that a fairly simple, direct connection ought to exist between social structure, class ideologies, and political parties. Many explanations of this putative connection exist, some mutually exclusive. Poverty is sometimes seen as a barrier to radicalism, sometimes as its most powerful spur; social mobility is sometimes said to increase, sometimes to decrease class awareness; ethnic cohesiveness is seen as an impediment to class solidarity or as the springboard from which it emerges. But whatever the specific argument, disproportionate influence is too often assigned to a single element of the social structure, and politics and ideology are too often viewed as simple reflections of economic relationships.

Particularly in the case of the United States, the conflation of class, society, and politics has unfortunate consequences. One cannot assume that the absence of a powerful social democratic party implies that American workers fully accept the status quo (although, as we shall see, such an assumption is often made). Actually, what needs to be explained is the coexistence in American history of workplace militancy and a politics organized around nonideological parties that appeal to broad coalitions rather than the interests of a particular class. David Montgomery has expressed the problem succinctly: "American

workers in the nineteenth century engaged in economic conflicts with their employers as fierce as any known to the industrial world; yet in their political behavior they consistently failed
to exhibit a class consciousness." Why was militancy in the factory so rarely translated into the politics of class? Labor and
socialist parties have emerged in the United States (indeed,
Americans, in the late 1820s, created the first "Workingmen's
parties" in the world), but they have tended to be locally oriented and short-lived. As Montgomery observes, the American
form of socialism has centered on gaining control of the workplace rather than on creating a working-class presence in politics.[3] "Why is there no socialism?" thus becomes a problem of
explaining the *disjuncture* of industrial relations and political
practice in the United States.

Finally, there is the problem of proposed answers that simply explain too much. Descriptions of an unchanging American ideology, or timeless aspects of the American social order
such as mobility, leave little room for understanding the powerful American radical tradition that was based upon cross-class
movements and appeals to moral sentiment rather than upon
economic interest. Nor can they explain those periods when
socialist politics did attract widespread support. It is too infre-
quently noted that at the time Sombart wrote, there *was*, in fact,
socialism in the United States. In the first fifteen years of this
century, the American Socialist party appeared to rival those in
Europe, except the German, in mass support and prospects for
future growth. Around 1910, the American Socialist party had
elected more officials than its English counterpart. Certainly,
Sombart's question might as readily have been asked about
Britain as the United States before World War I. Thus, what
must be explained is not simply why socialism is today absent

from American politics, but why it once rose and fell. Such a definition of the question, I will argue, requires that we "historicize" the problem of American socialism. Rather than assuming an unchanging pattern of American exceptionalism, we need to examine the key periods when American development diverged most markedly from that of Europe.

With these admonitions in mind, let us review some of the most prominent explanations for the weakness of socialism in the United States. Probably the most straightforward approach is the contention that the failure of socialism results from the success of American capitalism. Various aspects of the American social order, according to this argument, have led workers to identify their interests with the socioeconomic status quo. This, indeed, was the burden of Sombart's own analysis. The economic condition of workers in the United States, he insisted, was far better than that of Europeans in terms of wages, housing, and diet. Socially, moreover, they were far less sharply distinguished from the middle class than their European counterparts. And finally, they were conscious of being able to move west if dissatisfied with their present conditions. The success of capitalism, Sombart believed, made the American worker "a sober, calculating businessman, without ideals." "On the reefs of roast beef and apple pie," he added, "socialistic utopias of every sort are sent to their doom."[4]

From Frederick Jackson Turner's "frontier thesis," which saw in the westward movement the key to American distinctiveness, to more recent studies attributing the failure of socialism to high rates of geographical and social mobility and the ability of American workers to acquire property, the success of capitalism has been seen as making the American working class complacent and rendering socialism irrelevant to American politics. As anyone who has lived in both American and western Europe can testify, extremely high rates of geographical mobility are a distinctive feature of American life. In the nineteenth century, each decade witnessed a wholesale turnover of population in working-class neighborhoods, presumably with adverse effects on the possibility of creating permanent class institutions.[5] Even today, the lure of the Sunbelt draws workers from the depressed industrial heartland, an example of the individual "safety-valve" that Turner identified as the alternative to class conflict in the United States. A recent variant on the theme was the contention, popular during the 1960s, that the white working class had exchanged material security and a privileged status in relation to minorities at home and workers abroad for a renunciation of economic and political radicalism. Socialism, according to this view, could come to the United States only as the indirect result of revolutions in the Third World, or the activity of marginal social groups like migrant workers and welfare mothers not yet absorbed into the American mainstream.

Plausible as they appear, the "success of capitalism" and "social mobility" approaches raise as many questions as they answer. First, they rest upon assumptions about the standard of living of American workers that are rarely subjected to empirical verification. Have the wage levels and rates of social mobility of American workers always been significantly higher than in western Europe? Vague references to the "scarcity of labor" in the United States do not suffice to answer that question.[6] Many immigrants complained that certain aspects of their lives—the length of the workday, the pace of factory labor—compared unfavorably with conditions at home.

More importantly, the precise implications of the ability to acquire property for class consciousness and socialism are far more problematical than is often assumed. A venerable tradition of analysis, dating back at least as far as Alexis de Tocqueville, insists that far from promoting political stability, social mobility is a destabilizing force, raising expectations faster than they can be satisfied and thus encouraging demands for further change. Certainly, recent American and European studies of labor history suggest that the better-off workers—artisans in the nineteenth century, skilled factory workers in the twentieth—were most likely to take the lead in union organizing and radical politics.[7] As for geographical mobility, until historians are able to generalize about the success or failure of those millions who have, over the decades, left American farms and cities in search of economic opportunity, the implications of the extraordinary turbulence of the American population must remain an open question.[8] But in any case, the historian must beware of the temptation simply to deduce political ideology from social statistics or to assign disproportionate influence to a single aspect of the social structure. And finally, the "success of capitalism" formula can hardly explain the relative weakness of socialism during the Great Depression, which failed to produce a mass-based socialist movement, or the radicalism of the 1960s, which arose in a period of unparalleled affluence.

Even more popular than the "social mobility" thesis is the contention that the very ethos of American life is inherently hostile to class consciousness, socialism, and radicalism of any kind. Probably the best-known expression of this point of view is Louis Hartz's *The Liberal Tradition in America*. To summarize

Hartz's argument very briefly, Americans were "born equal," never having had to launch a revolution to obtain political democracy or social equality, with the result that American ideology has been dominated by a Lockean, individualistic outlook against which neither socialism on the left nor serious conservatism on the right can make any headway. A thoroughly bourgeois "fragment" spun off by Europe, America possessed only one part of the European social order. Lacking a hereditary aristocracy and a dispossessed working class, it had no need for class ideologies and politics.

No feudalism, no socialism. This oft-repeated aphorism sums up Hartz's contention that socialism arises from a vision, inherited from the feudal past, of a society based upon a structure of fixed orders and classes. Without a feudal tradition or a sense of class oppression in the present, Americans are simply unable to think in class terms. Indeed, in its ideals of social mobility, individual fulfillment, and material acquisitiveness, American ideology produced a utopia more compelling than anything socialism could offer. Socialists called for a classless society; Americans, according to Hartz, were convinced they already lived in one.[9]

Dominant in the 1950s, the "consensus" school of American historiography exemplified by Hartz has lately been supplanted by an interpretation of the American past that is marked less by ideological agreement than by persistent conflict among various racial and ethnic groups and social classes. The rise of the new social and labor history, and a new sensitivity to the historical experience of blacks, women, and others ignored in Hartz's formulation, has made historians extremely wary of broad generalizations about a unitary "American ideology." The work of Hartz, Richard Hofstadter, and others appears to a generation of historians who came of age during the turmoil of the 1960s as excessively celebratory of the American experience. Actually, like Hofstadter's *The American Political Tradition*, the first major expression of the "consensus" interpretation, *The Liberal Tradition* was not a celebration of American distinctiveness at all but a devastating critique of a political culture incapable of producing anything approaching an original idea. There was a right-wing bias in much "consensus" writing (represented, for example, by Daniel Boorstin, who gloried in the native pragmatism that, he contended, enabled Americans to escape the disruptive political ideologies of Europe). But Hartz and Hofstadter, who shared Marxist backgrounds, believed America's imprisonment within the confines of liberal ideology rendered it incapable of understanding the social realities of the modern world. They were concerned less with socialism and its failure than with affirming the underlying unities on which the American experience was girded, and with supplying a corrective to older interpretations that had mistaken the family quarrels of American political parties for ideological struggles over the nature of American society.[10]

The work of the new labor and social history, as I have indicated, has battered the "consensus" interpretation. In contrast to the universal diffusion of liberal values, students of working-class culture have stressed the development of semiautonomous working-class and ethnic cultures resting on an ethic of community and mutuality rather than individualism and competition.[11] The idea of an unchallenged bourgeois hegemony is also weakened when one considers that until the Civil War, the most powerful political class in the United States was composed of Southern slaveholding planters, a group that was bourgeois neither in its relationship to labor nor in its social ideology. Although the Old South was hardly "feudal" (a term Hartz invokes without providing a precise definition), it was certainly pre-bourgeois in many respects. One might almost suggest that with its aristocratic social order and disenfranchised laboring class, the South should, if Hartz is correct, have provided fertile soil for socialism.[12]

Hartz's thesis has also been weakened from an entirely different direction: intellectual history. Recent writing on eighteenth-century American ideology has not simply dethroned Locke from the pivotal ideological role accorded him by Hartz but has virtually expelled him from the pantheon of early American thought. The political rhetoric of the American Revolution, according to recent studies, owed less to Lockean liberalism than to classical republicanism, an ideology that defined the pursuit of individual self-interest as a repudiation of that "virtue" (devotion to the public good) indispensable in a republican citizenry. Eventually, liberalism triumphed as the dominant rhetoric of American political culture, but not until well into the nineteenth century and as the result of a historical process whose outlines remain unclear. But if Hartz's liberal consensus did not characterize all of American history, then other elements of his argument, such as the absence of a feudal past, lose much of their explanatory power. The notion of an overarching liberal consensus went far toward explaining the context within which Hartz wrote—America of the 1950s—but has proved of little value in accounting for the strength of challenges to the capitalist order ranging from the class violence of 1877 to the Knights of Labor, populism, and the old Socialist party.[13]

Nonetheless, Hartz's contention that even American radicals have been trapped within a liberal ideology devoted to the defense of individualism and private property is not entirely incompatible with recent studies of the radical tradition. From Tom Paine's studied distinction between society and government (the former an unmixed blessing, the latter a necessary evil), to abolitionists' critique of all social and political relationships embodying coercion, to the American anarchists whose individualist outlook differed so markedly from the class-oriented anarchist movements of Europe, a potent strand of the American radical tradition has rested upon hostility to the state and the defense of the free individual. The ideologies of nineteenth-century labor and farmers' movements, and even early-twentieth-century socialism itself, owed more to traditional republican notions of the equal citizen and the independent small producer than to the coherent analysis of class-divided society.

Precapitalist culture, it appears, was the incubator of resistance to capitalist development in the United States. The world of the artisan and small farmer persisted in some parts of the country into the twentieth century and powerfully influenced American radical movements. The hallmarks of labor and populist rhetoric were demands for "equal rights," antimonopoly, land reform, and an end to the exploitation of producers by nonproducers. These movements inherited an older republican tradition that was hostile to large accumulations of property but that viewed small property as the foundation of economic and civic autonomy. Perhaps we ought to stand Hartz on his head. Not the *absence* of nonliberal ideas but the *persistence* of a radical vision resting on small property inhibited the rise of socialist ideologies. Recent studies of American socialism itself, indeed, stress the contrast between native-born socialists, whose outlook relied heavily on the older republican tradition, and more class-conscious immigrant socialists. According to Nick Salvatore, American socialists like Eugene V. Debs viewed corporate capitalism, not socialism, as the revolutionary force in American life, disrupting local communities, undermining the ideal of the independent citizen, and introducing class divisions into a previously homogenous social order.[14]

Salvatore and other recent writers are not reverting to a "consensus" view of American history, though their work explores the values that native-born socialists shared with other Americans. But ironically, at the same time that one group of historians strongly influenced by the radicalism of the 1960s was dismantling the "consensus" view of the American past, another was resurrecting it as a theory of the "hegemony" of middle-class or capitalist values in the United States. In one version of the "consensus"/"hegemony" approach, labor and capital were seen as united by an ideology of "corporate liberalism" that, beneath an antibusiness veneer, served the interests of the existing order. Government regulation of the economy, hailed by American reformers as a means of blunting capitalist rapaciousness and seen by many radicals as a stepping-stone to a fully planned economy and perhaps even socialism itself, was now interpreted as the vehicle through which capitalists were able to control the political economy without appearing to do so. Because of the resiliency of corporate liberalism, virtually all popular protest movements had been incorporated within the expanding capitalist order.[15]

A somewhat different version of the "hegemony" argument emphasizes culture rather than political ideology. The rise of mass culture, the mass media, and mass consumption in twentieth-century America, according to this view, not only rendered obsolete the socialist goal of building an alternative culture within capitalist society but shaped the aspirations of workers, making leisure and consumption, rather than work or politics, the yardsticks of personal fulfillment. Recent studies of nineteenth- and early-twentieth-century American radical movements have focused not on such traditional concerns as political ideology and organizational history but on the creation of "countercultures" within the larger society. Obviously influenced by the theory of hegemony (and in some cases, by a perhaps idealized understanding of the much-publicized cultural activities of the modern Italian Communist party), these works have implied that the seedbed of socialist politics is a counterhegemonic set of cultural institutions rather than the polity or the workplace. But studies of the modern working class have emphasized the disintegration of "working-class culture." "Social life," contends one such analysis, "is no longer organized around the common relation to the production of both culture and commodities. The working class public sphere is dead."[16]

Unfortunately, the "consensus" interpretation in its radical "hegemony" variants still suffers from the problem of homogenizing the American past and present. Indeed, in adopting the notion of hegemony from Gramsci, American historians have often transformed it from a subtle mode of exploring the ways class struggle is muted and channeled in modern society, into a substitute for social conflict. The sophisticated analysis of a writer like Raymond Williams, who observes how diverse ideologies can survive even in the face of apparent "hegemony," is conspicuously absent from American writing.[17] The notion that mass culture and mass society render any kind of resistance impossible, moreover, can hardly explain the dissatisfactions reflected in the radicalism of the 1960s. In the end, the "hegemony" argument too often ends up being circular. Rather than being demonstrated, the "hegemony" of mass culture and liberal values is inferred from the "absence" of protest, and then this absence is attributed to the self-same "hegemony."

An entirely different set of answers to the "why is there no socialism" question derives from the sociology of the working class itself and examines aspects of the American social order that make it difficult for workers to organize successfully. The assumption is that socialist politics is unlikely to emerge in the face of an internally divided working class. The traditional assumption that capitalist development must produce an increasingly homogenous proletariat with a single set of interests, represented by unions and a political party, has given way before a recognition of the many kinds of divisions and stratifications built into the capitalist labor process itself. Divisions between the skilled and unskilled, craft and industrial workers, often reinforced by divisions along lines of race, ethnicity, and gender, belie the notion of a unified working class. It is doubtful, however, that such divisions are very useful in explaining the unique features of American labor history, for it appears that similar segmentation exists in other advanced capitalist societies. The United States is hardly the only country where capitalist development has failed to produce a homogenous working class.[18]

Even more common than labor market segmentation as an explanation for the distinctive history of the American working class is its racial and ethnic heterogeneity. The complex web of backgrounds from which the American proletariat emerged is often seen as rendering unity along class lines all but impossible. Although apparently straightforward, the notion that the exceptional diversity of the American working class has inhibited both class consciousness and socialist politics actually encompasses a number of distinct approaches to American labor history.

On the simplest level, it is easy to point to the critical role that racism and ethnic prejudices have played in shaping the history of American labor. For most of American history, black workers were systematically excluded from unions. On the West Coast, prejudice against the Chinese shaped the labor movement, helping to solidify the domination of conservative skilled craft workers over a less skilled majority. The racism of many labor organizations in turn fostered prejudice against unions among minority workers.[19] And even in the case of white ethnic groups, differences of language, culture, and tradition clearly made organization difficult early in this century, when massive immigration from southern and eastern Europe coincided with the rapid expansion and consolidation of monopoly capitalism. The constant redefinition and re-creation of American labor (a process that continues today with new waves of immigration) also meant that working-class institutions and traditions had to be rebuilt and battles refought over and over again. "The making of the American working class" (a subject yet to find its historian) was a process that occurred many times rather than once.

The diverse backgrounds from which the American working class was forged is sometimes seen as affecting class consciousness in other ways as well. Racial and ethnic loyalties often drew men and women into cross-class alliances, while racism, nativism, and ethnic hostilities inherited from Europe all inhibited the development of a consciousness of workers' collective interests. Immigrant groups created a complex network of ethnic social, religious, and political institutions, diverting working-class energies from institutions like unions and radical political parties that explicitly sought to unite men and women across ethnic lines.[20] Others contend that the cultural heritage of Catholic immigrants, who comprised a large portion of the industrial working class, made them unreceptive to any form of political radicalism. In his pioneering study of Irish immigrants in nineteenth-century Boston, Oscar Handlin portrayed a religious community that saw efforts to change the world as at best futile and at worst sacrilegious. Handlin's argument has sometimes been generalized to the proposition that ex-peasant immigrants are inherently indifferent or hostile to radical movements. (This contention begs the question of why, for instance, groups like Italian immigrants played so prominent a role in the creation of the labor and socialist movements in Argentina, while allegedly eschewing radicalism in the United States.) Another line of argument derives from the large numbers of early-twentieth-century "new immigrants" (Italians, Poles, Greeks, and others) who were actually migrant laborers, planning only a brief stay in the United States. In 1910, for example, three-quarters as many Italians left for home as entered the United States. Not intending to make the United States a permanent haven, Gerald Rosenblum argues, these new immigrants reinforced the narrow "business" orientation of American labor organizations: higher wages, not efforts at social change, were what attracted them to unions.[21]

Despite the popularity of what might be called the "ethnic" explanation for the weakness of American socialism, it is by no means clear that cultural divisions were an insuperable barrier to class consciousness or political socialism. Racism and ethnic prejudice are not, as they are sometimes treated, "transhistorical" phenomena that exist independently of historical time and place. What needs to be studied is what kind of organizing and what conditions have allowed unions to overcome preexisting prejudices. Unions organized on an industrial basis have under certain circumstances been able to bring black and white workers together. The Industrial Workers of the World managed to lead successful militant strikes early in this century by recognizing that ethnicity can, under certain circumstances, generate distinctive forms of radical protest. This is especially true where class and ethnic lines coincide, as in turn-of-the-century American industrial communities. Ethnic group solidarity, Victor Greene has argued, actually increased militancy during strikes by immigrant workers in the Pennsylvania coal fields, and the IWW's tactic of establishing strike committees composed of democratically elected representatives from each ethnic group, brought to its strikes all the strength of the preexisting network of immigrant institutions. So long as each group believed no one group was receiving favored treatment, the bonds of ethnicity in no way contradicted a willingness to work with others.[22] Like many "global" explanations for the failure of socialism, in other words, the "ethnic" approach proves too much: rather than investigating the specific circumstances under which radical and ethnic divisions inhibit class solidarity, it assumes that a diverse working class can never achieve unity in economic or political action.[23]

Related to the composition of the American working class, of course, is the distinctive character of American trade unionism itself. Why, despite a history of labor violence unparalleled in Europe, does organized labor in the United States appear so much more conservative and apolitical than its European counterparts? Sometimes attention is drawn to the exclusionary policies of American Federation of Labor unions, whose craft basis of organization reinforced preexisting divisions between skilled and unskilled workers and excluded large numbers of workers—blacks, women, new immigrants, and others—from the labor movement. Indeed, it has been argued by James O'Connor that, in a nation in which a majority of the workforce has never belonged to trade unions, the higher wages of unionized workers are, in effect, subsidized by lower-paid nonunion workers via inflation. Other writers contend that the problem is not the nature and role of unions per se but the fact that labor leaders have constantly sought to undercut the militancy of the rank and file, preferring accommodations with capital to prolonged class struggle. Whether this is a question of the perfidy of individual "misleaders" or the growth of bureaucratic structures isolating officials from their membership, the result has been a union movement uninterested in posing a political challenge to capital.

No one, however, has satisfactorily explained how and why a presumably militant rank and file constantly chooses moderate "misleaders" to represent it. And it should be noted that the implicit portrait of class-conscious workers betrayed again and again by a corrupt or moderate leadership assumes a unity and militancy among American workers that other approaches to the "failure of socialism" question have discounted. One might, in fact, argue that at a number of points in American history, the image of a moderate leadership curbing a radical rank and file ought to be reversed. In the 1930s, for example, it is now clear that socialist and communist organizers played a pivotal role in galvanizing working-class protest and creating the Congress of Industrial Organizations (CIO) industrial unions.[24]

Thus far we have considered approaches to the question of socialism that focus upon the society or the workplace. An alternative point of view looks to the nature of the American political system, since it is a political party whose absence is to be explained. Various aspects of American politics, it is argued, have made it difficult for labor or socialist parties to establish themselves effectively. First, there is the early achievement of political democracy in the United States, the "free gift of the ballot," as Selig Perlman termed it. Unlike the situation in Europe, the vast majority of male American workers enjoyed the suffrage well before the advent of the industrial revolution. In England, class consciousness was catalyzed, at least in part, by the struggle for the vote; the exclusion of workers from the suffrage paralleled and reinforced the sense of a class-divided society learned at the workplace. In the United States, however, the "lessons" of the polity were the opposite of those of the economy. In the latter, the worker often perceived himself as an equal citizen of the republic. Alan Dawley, indeed, writes that "the ballot box was the coffin of class consciousness" in nineteenth-century America. Not only were the major parties remarkably adept at absorbing labor leaders into political office, but the early achievement of political democracy (for white men) gave workers a vested interest in the existing political order. American workers, according to this argument, developed a strong sense of their "rights" in both polity and workplace but were not convinced of the necessity of launching a direct national political challenge to capital. Perhaps labor parties never advanced beyond the local level in the United States because workers did not see the national state as being under the control of a hostile class. And even on the local level, Ira Katznelson argues, workers traditionally allocated economic issues to unions, while politics centered not on questions of class but rather on the distribution of patronage among competing ethnic groups by urban political machines.[25]

The unusual structure of American politics has also affected the possibilities for socialist parties. The winner-take-all Electoral College method of choosing the president helps entrench the two-party system (since votes cast for a third candidate who cannot achieve a majority in a state are "wasted"). The size and regional diversity of the country has made it difficult to translate local labor strength into national power. American political parties have proven remarkably adept at absorbing protest, adopting the demands of reformers in watered-down form, and forcing radicals to choose in elections between the lesser of two evils. The contrast between the American 1930s, when Franklin D. Roosevelt's New Deal made broad concessions to labor and thereby cemented an alliance with the union movement, and the conservative policies of Depression-era British governments is only one example of the remarkable flexibility of American parties. To liberal historians, such actions vindicate the receptivity of the American political order to demands for reform; to radicals they often appear as frustrating barriers to truly far-reaching change.[26]

Other political factors have also inhibited the rise of labor and socialist politics. American historians have yet to assess the full implications of the disenfranchisement of Southern blacks from the late nineteenth century until the 1960s. Here was a

group comprising a significant portion of the American working class that, when given the opportunity, proved receptive to
parties like the populists that sought far-reaching changes in
American life. Their exclusion from political participation
shifted American politics to the right while entrenching within
the Democratic party a powerful bloc of Southern reactionar-
ies. At various times, immigrants and most migrant laborers
have also been barred from voting. Industrial workers, moreover, have never formed anything approaching a majority of
the American electorate. In a vast nation, predominantly rural
until well into the twentieth century, parties resting exclusively
upon labor could not hope to win national power. In 1900, the
United States was already the world's foremost industrial
power, yet a majority of the population still lived in places with
fewer than twenty-five hundred residents.

A final "political" consideration, often stressed by historians
sympathetic to American socialism but minimized by those
who are not, is outright repression. The populists were deprived
of electoral victories throughout the South by blatant fraud in
the 1890s. Violence by federal and state troops and private
police forces suppressed strikes on many occasions, and court
injunctions defeated many others. The first Red Scare of
1919–20, which jailed and deported radical leaders, devastated
both the Socialist party and the IWW. The second, after World
War II, effectively destroyed the Communist party.[27]

Each of these "political" approaches contains an element of
plausibility, but many suffer from a shortcoming shared by other
explanations for the failure of socialism: they invoke aspects of
American politics that are common to other countries to
explain American exceptionalism. To take one example, virtually every European socialist movement suffered governmental

repression at one time or another in its history, sometimes far more severe repression than anything experienced in the United States. (Very few American radicals, after all, were executed by the state.) The Spanish labor and communist movements suffered under Franco, the Italian under Mussolini; German socialists faced Bismarck's antisocialist laws. Yet all managed to survive, and some emerged stronger than ever. The 1919 and post–World War II Red Scares were not confined to the United States. Why, one may ask, has repression proved more effective against radicals in the United States than elsewhere? Of course, one might argue that the very openness of American politics, the normalcy of democratic procedures, makes it difficult for radical movements to deal with repression when it does appear. American radicals, because of the democratic political culture from which they have emerged, have lacked the tradition of underground organization that might have enabled them to survive repressive governments. Of course, one might also ask why, if the state has been unusually repressive in the United States, American workers have persisted in viewing the national government as somehow being above class politics.

Other political explanations also leave important questions unanswered. The Electoral College system biases American politics toward a two-party system but does not explain why socialists have been unable to replace the Republicans or Democrats with a socialist or labor party (as the Republicans replaced the Whigs in the 1850s). The fact that industrial workers form a minority of the total population is hardly unique to the United States. Socialist and labor parties everywhere have come to power by appealing to middle-class and rural voters as well as industrial laborers. In every industrial country, moreover, a considerable minority of workers have always voted for nonsocialist parties. The implicit comparison between a class-conscious European working class and the politically fragmented American proletariat may not stand up to careful scrutiny of European political history.

Thus far, the answers to the socialism problem have been largely "external"—they have emphasized aspects of American society and politics that have inhibited the growth of socialist politics and working-class consciousness. There are also explanations that might be described as "internal"—those that focus on the nature and presumed errors of radical movements themselves. Such an approach has an obvious appeal for more optimistic left-oriented historians. For if essentially unchanging aspects of American society—social mobility, the "American ideology," the nature of the political system—are responsible for the failure of socialism, there appears to be little reason to hope for a future revival of socialist fortunes. If, however, tactical, strategic, or ideological errors sabotaged previous socialist movements, then perhaps future radicals can learn from past mistakes, avoid repeating them, and rebuild American socialism.

The "internal" approach also has the virtue of directing attention to the actual histories of past socialist movements and the specific circumstances that contributed to their rise and fall. After all, if one accepts as sufficient an "external" explanation, one need not study in any detail the history of particular attempts to create a socialist politics in the United States. The "internal" approach, in other words, tends to "historicize" the socialism question, forcing the historian to examine the specific contingencies that affected the failure of socialist parties rather than advancing generalizations about American society so sweeping as almost to stand outside history itself. Not surprisingly, the two periods of American history that have attracted the most attention from those interested in tracing the history of past socialisms are the first two decades of the twentieth century and the 1930s and 1940s. Both stand out as eras when the trajectory of socialist movements in the United States diverged most markedly from that of their European counterparts. Why did the American Socialist and Communist parties fail to build upon their undoubted successes and establish themselves as permanent parts of the country's body politic?

One kind of "internal" approach, associated most prominently with Daniel Bell, argues that American socialists and communists failed to attract broad support because of their sectarian orientation and concern with ideological purity rather than with the give-and-take essential to success in American politics. "In the world but not of it," they eschewed reforms in favor of a preoccupation with socialist revolution, thereby isolating themselves more or less by choice. A somewhat analogous argument is that of James Weinstein, who begins by challenging Bell's portrait of the Socialist party, insisting that between 1900 and 1919 it acted as a traditional reformist party, taking ideology less seriously than the winning of votes. In the end, however, according to Weinstein, the party succumbed to the kind of ideological rigidity described by Bell, exemplified by the attempt of one faction, allied with the Comintern, to impose the Soviet model of a highly disciplined, ideologically correct party on what had been a broad coalition in the mainstream of American politics.[28]

Despite its success in winning local elections (the Socialist party by 1912 had elected some twelve hundred local officials and thirty-three state legislators and controlled municipal governments in such cities as Schenectady, Milwaukee, and Berkeley) and attracting a respectable vote for Eugene V. Debs for president in 1912 (900,000 ballots, or six percent of the electorate), the Socialist party suffered from a number of internal weaknesses. Paul Buhle stresses the nativism of many party leaders and their unwillingness to reach out to the new immigrant proletariat. The party's electoral obsession, which led it to measure the advance of socialism almost solely in terms of the ballot box, led it to neglect organizing when votes were not at stake. Preoccupied with electoral strategies, the party failed to respond to the massive upheaval of unskilled immigrant factory workers between 1909 and 1919. Where was the Socialist party at McKees Rocks, Lawrence, or the great steel strike of 1919? The Industrial Workers of the World demonstrated that it was possible to organize the new immigrant proletariat, but despite sympathy for the IWW on the part of Debs and other left-wing socialists, the two organizations went their separate ways. Here, indeed, was the underlying tragedy of those years: the militancy expressed in the IWW was never channeled for political purposes, while socialist politics ignored the immigrant workers. Indeed, the Socialist party's strength lay not among factory workers but in an unusual amalgam of native-born small farmers, skilled workers in certain cities, ethnic groups from the Russian Empire like Finns and Jews, and professionals and intellectuals. Leon Trotsky was perhaps unkind when he remarked that the American Socialists were "a party of dentists." But its thinness among the industrial working class was certainly among the party's most debilitating weaknesses.[29]

Another explanation for the decline of American socialism focuses on the crisis brought about by World War I. The Socialist party's principled opposition to America's participation in the war fundamentally transformed it, alienating many native-born members and intellectuals while attracting a new constituency among immigrant workers. Ironically, at the moment of its final collapse, the Socialist party for the first time accurately reflected the composition of the American proletariat.

Opposition to the war laid the party open to the massive repression that was, at least in part, responsible for its demise. One may speculate whether, had American Socialists, like their European counterparts, supported the war and perhaps even entered a coalition wartime government as a junior partner, as the Labour party in Britain did, they might have shielded themselves from repression and established their political legitimacy. (Of course, one may well ask whether participation in governing an imperialist nation involves a socialist party in an inevitable sacrifice of principle, at least so far as foreign policy is concerned.) What is clear is an outcome fraught with irony, in view of the assumption that American socialism is so much weaker than that of Europe. Of the two great "isms" created by the nineteenth century—socialism and nationalism—the latter in western Europe proved far the stronger in 1914. Socialist internationalism was crucified on the cross of socialist support for the war effort. Was the American party's opposition to the war a courageous act of suicide? At least, history ought to record that the American Socialist party went to its death not because there was *less* socialism in the United States than in Europe, but because, apart from the Russian Bolsheviks, the American was the party that remained most true to socialist principles.

If the period before World War I represented one opportunity for the development of a mass socialist party in the United

States, the 1930s appears to represent another. By the mid-1930s, the Communist party had established itself as the major force on the socialist left. The achievements of the communists, recent research has made clear, were indeed impressive. Moving far beyond the electoral emphasis of the old Socialist party, they understood that struggle, on a variety of fronts, is the most effective means of mass mobilization and education. In contrast to the socialists' isolation from the militant struggles of the pre–World War I years, the communists took the lead in a remarkable array of activities—union-building, demonstrations of the unemployed, civil rights agitation, aid to republican Spain, and so on. Indeed, the wide variety of their activities becomes all the more amazing when it is remembered that the party at its prewar peak numbered well under 100,000 members.[30]

Given the mass militancy of the CIO and the range of party concerns, why did a larger socialist or labor political presence not emerge from the Great Depression? Some accounts stress the resiliency of the political system itself, the way President Roosevelt managed to absorb labor militancy into a reconfigured Democratic party coalition. Others point to the internecine warfare between AFL and CIO unions as sabotaging efforts toward the creation of an independent labor party. Still others blame the Communist party's quest for legitimacy, especially in its Popular Front period. The party's determination to forge an alliance of all antifascist elements, including the Democratic party, and its ideological emphasis upon American nationalism ("Communism is twentieth-century Americanism," as the mid-1930s slogan went), foreclosed the possibility of independent socialist politics. According to James Weinstein, here also lay a cardinal difference between the old socialists, who at least had made socialism a part of American political discourse, and the 1930s communists, who saw themselves as the left wing of the New Deal coalition.[31]

But like the old Socialist party, the communists were unable to cut the Gordian knot of the relationship between nationalism and socialism. On the one hand, the party achieved primacy on the left partially by virtue of its relationship with the USSR, the only existing socialist state. On the other, the Soviet connection proved a point of vulnerability, opening the party to repression as "un-American" after World War II and leading to inevitable questions as to whether specific policies reflected American or Soviet interests and realities. It is not clear, however, how much emphasis ought to be put on the Soviet connection for the party's failure to grow in size. After all, every Communist party in the world had to deal with the Comintern. What is certain is that the CP was most successful precisely when it was most American. As Maurice Isserman demonstrates, the Popular Front, whatever its relationship to socialist ideology, was exactly the policy that most American communists desired, and the party's membership was highest in the mid-1930s and again toward the end of World War II, precisely when socialism and nationalism coincided. Indeed, recent studies of the war years criticize the party for subordinating labor militancy to the war effort and a quest for nationalist legitimacy, via the no-strike pledge.[32] (The implicit assumption that calls for greater efforts to win the war alienated American workers concerned only with their paychecks may, however, be open to question.)

Through the no-strike pledge, its subordination of criticism of the Roosevelt administration, and the decision to transform itself from a party into a "political association," the Communist party sought "legitimacy"—a permanent foothold in American politics—during World War II. The experience of war and the resistance movements did legitimize European communist parties as defenders of their nations. (No one, whatever his political outlook, could call the French or Italian Communist parties "un-French" or "un-Italian" after the experience of World War II.) But American communists ended up with the worst of both worlds. The no-strike pledge alienated shop-floor militants without winning "legitimacy" from those with the power to dispense it—the price, perhaps, of trying to exist at all at the very focal point of world imperialism. The party remained vulnerable to the wave of repression that began with the onset of the cold war. The base that communists had laboriously created in the labor movement was effectively destroyed, with disastrous consequences for the militancy of the postwar labor movement.

Let us return, in conclusion, to our original question. Why is there no socialism in the United States? As we have seen, all the explanations that have been proposed—the internal and the external, the social, ideological, economic, and cultural—have a certain merit, and all seem to have weaknesses as well. Nor can we simply add them all together in a kind of mixed salad and feel satisfied with the result. Perhaps the debate has gone on for so long and so inconclusively because the question itself is fundamentally flawed. Perhaps beginning our investigation with a negative question inevitably invites ahistorical answers.

Like a kindred question that has bedeviled the study of American slavery—"Why were there no slave rebellions in the United States?"—the socialism question rests on a number of assumptions that may not survive careful analysis. The rise of socialism, or the outbreak of a slave rebellion, is defined as a normal occurrence, whose absence requires explanation. In

141

the case of slavery, the question is premised upon the conviction that the "normal" human response to severe repression is armed rebellion, an assumption for which human history, unfortunately, does not offer much support. In the case of socialism, the premise is that under capitalism, the working class will inevitably develop class consciousness, expressed in unions and a labor or socialist political party, and that consequently the failure of each to emerge must be the result of some outside interference. No one asks, for example, "Why is there no feminism in Europe?" (a legitimate question when either independent feminist movements or the historical participation of women in socialist parties in Europe and the United States are compared), because socialism is held to be an inevitable, universal development under capitalism while feminism is assumed to emerge from local contingencies that vary from country to country.

In the end, of course, "Why is there no socialism?" rests upon an interpretation of history that accords socialism a privileged position among radical movements because it arises inexorably out of the inner logic of capitalist development and holds out the promise of a far-reaching social revolution. But it seems to me that the empirical evidence that justifies the question—the existence of mass labor, socialist, and communist parties in western Europe and not in the United States—fundamentally contradicts the Marxist foundation of the question. For the "absence" to be explained is not socialism (a revolutionary transformation of society) but the existence of political parties of a decidedly social democratic bent that aim at no such transformation. The left parties of western Europe have without doubt improved the conditions of life of their constituents, but they have proved incapable of using their impressive political strength to fundamentally reshape their societies. They have, one might say, promoted liberalism and egalitarianism more successfully than socialism and presented themselves as the proponents of modernization and social rationalization rather than class rule, thus operating in ways more analogous to American political parties than either Americans or Europeans would care to admit. The issue for western European socialist parties is not precisely socialism but the equitable distribution of the products of capitalism. In other words, one might well ask not "Why is there no socialism in the United States?" but "Why has there been no socialist transformation in any advanced capitalist society?"

To put the question this way challenges another underlying premise of the socialism question: American exceptionalism. Too often in American historical writing, "Europe" is posited as an unchanging class-conscious monolith in contrast to the liberal, bourgeois United States. In much American writing, "Europe" equals France, and "France" equals the French Revolution. The heroic struggles of European workers and socialists are highlighted, and the more recent erosion of working-class consciousness and socialist ideology ignored. Too often American historians equate the official doctrine of "revolutionary" labor movements, such as the French earlier in this century, or political platforms calling for collective ownership of the means of production, with a pervasive socialist consciousness among a majority of workers. They ignore the fact that large numbers of European workers have always voted for "bourgeois" parties. American commentators often cite the history of British labor as one example of class-conscious "European" working-class development, unaware of the debates among British writers about what some see as an exceptional *absence* of socialism compared with the continent. Certainly, recent events demonstrate that "the containment of . . . working-class movements within the limits of trade union economism and social democratic reformism" is hardly unique to the United States.[33]

To abandon American exceptionalism as an organizing theme is not, of course, to assert that the history of every capitalist nation is identical. The history of the United States is, in important ways, unique, as is that of England, France, Germany, and every other country. But a preoccupation with the exceptional elements of the American experience obscures those common patterns and processes that transcend national boundaries, most notably the global expansion of capitalism in the nineteenth and twentieth centuries and its political and ideological ramifications. It also diverts attention from the "Americanizing" influences so prominent in western Europe during the past generation. America, Sombart wrote, was "the land of our future." Are not the economies, and the working classes, of both America and Europe today being transformed by the decline of old basic industries, the backbone of traditional unionism and socialism? Is not European politics, like European popular culture, becoming more and more "American," with single-issue movements rising to prominence and political parties, even those calling themselves socialist, emphasizing the personalities of their leaders and their appeal to the entire electorate, rather than a carefully delineated ideology representing the interests of a particular social class? Western European socialist and communist parties today occupy points on the political spectrum ranging from distinctly moderate (the Italian, Danish, and Portuguese Socialist parties) to various shades of left, and some, like the British Labour party, are bitterly divided against themselves. In such a situation, it is not at all clear that "socialism" retains any clearly defined political content. Perhaps, because mass politics, mass culture, and mass consumption came to America before they came to Europe, American socialists were the first to face the dilemma of how to define socialist politics in a capitalist democracy. Perhaps, in the dissipation of class ideologies, Europe is now catching up with a historical process already experienced in the United States.[34] Perhaps future expressions of radicalism in Europe will embody less a traditional socialist ideology than an "American" appeal to libertarian and moral values and resistance to disabilities based upon race and gender. Or perhaps a continuing world economic crisis will propel politics both in western Europe and in America down a more class-oriented path. Only time will tell whether the United States has been behind Europe in the development of socialism, or ahead of it in socialism's decline.

PART III

THE ENDURING
CIVIL WAR

SEVEN

WHO IS AN AMERICAN?

In 1995, the New York Council for the Humanities selected me as its second Scholar of the Year. For my talk at the award ceremony, I chose to address a subject then at the center of a fierce national debate—the definition of American nationality.

This was a moment when the Republican party of California had embarked on an anti-immigrant crusade (with what turned out to be politically disastrous results), bilingual education in the nation's schools was under fierce attack by those proclaiming English the nation's "official" language, and the writer Peter Brimelow had received much attention for his book *Alien Nation,* which warned that nonwhite immigration was destroying America's "ethno-cultural community," a community grounded, he insisted, in shared European ancestry. At the same time, commentators were blaming the "new social history," which emphasizes the diverse experiences of the numerous groups that make up American society, for the loss of a sense of social unity and the fragmentation of national consciousness.

My talk traced this debate back to the nation's founding era and suggested that there was nothing new in disagreements and worries about American identity. The tension between inclusive and restrictive definitions of the national community has a long history. There has never been a single answer to the question "Who is an American?"

•

Americans have always had a highly ambiguous attitude toward history. "The past," wrote Herman Melville, "is the text-book of tyrants; the future is the Bible of the free." Yet like many other peoples, we have always looked to history for a sense of national cohesiveness. To a large extent, today's debates over history are inspired by concern over a perceived fragmentation of American society, a fear that modern scholarship emphasizes what divides Americans rather than what they share in common.

Historians should certainly seek to identify the common themes of American history. Yet these themes are not as one-dimensional or as easy to delineate as many critics of the "new history" suppose. Difference and commonality are both intrinsic parts of the American experience. The diverse groups that make up American society have long spoken a common political language, although they have often interpreted its vocabulary in very different ways. Apparently universal principles and common values, moreover, have been historically constructed on the basis of difference and exclusion.

Nowhere is this symbiotic relationship between inclusion and exclusion—between a national creed that emphasizes democracy and freedom as universal rights and a reality of limiting these entitlements to particular groups of people—more evident than in debates over that fundamental question "Who is an American?" Today many politicians blame America's problems on an alien invasion and propose to redefine our nationality along racial and ethnic lines. But there is nothing new in bitter conflicts about who should and should not be an American citizen. We as a people have long been obsessed with definitions of "Americanness."

A nation, in Benedict Anderson's celebrated definition, is more than a political entity. It is also a state of mind, "an imagined political community," with borders that are as much intellectual as geographic. Rather than being permanently fixed, national identities are inherently unstable, subject to continuing efforts to draw and redraw their imagined borders. Like democracy, freedom, equality, and other key words of our political language, "American" is what philosophers call an "essentially contested concept"—one that by its very nature is subject to multiple and conflicting interpretations.

In a society resting, rhetorically at least, on the ideal of equality, the boundaries of the imagined community take on extreme significance. Within the cognitive border, Americans have long assumed, civil and political equality ought to prevail, and the cry of "second-class citizenship" has provided a powerful language of social protest. The greater the substantive rights of American citizenship, the more important the boundaries of inclusion and exclusion. American history is not simply the story of a fixed set of rights to which one group after another has gained access. On the contrary, the definition of those rights has changed as a consequence of battles at the boundary, the demands of excluded groups for inclusion. For example, after the Civil War and again in the 1950s and 1960s, the struggle for full citizenship by former slaves and their descendants inspired similar claims by other groups and transformed what it is to be an American.

Americans' debates about the bases of our national identity reflect a larger contradiction in the Western tradition itself. For if the West, as we are frequently reminded, created the idea of "liberty" as a universal human right, it also invented the concept of "race" and ascribed to it predictive powers about human behavior. Nationalism, at least in America, is the child of both these beliefs. Traditionally, scholars have distinguished between civic nationalism, which envisions the nation as a community based on shared political institutions and values with membership open to all who reside within its territory, and ethnic nationalism, which considers a nation a community of descent based on a shared ethnic and linguistic heritage. France exemplifies the inclusive civic brand of nationhood, and Germany the exclusionary ethnic form. Most American scholars identify the United States with the French model. Since the time of independence, they argue, our raison d'être as a nation has rested on principles that are universal, not parochial; to be an American, all one had to do was commit oneself to an ideology of liberty, equality, and democracy.

In actual practice, however, American nationality has long combined both civic and ethnic definitions. For most of our history, American citizenship has been defined by blood as well as political allegiance. Both ideas can be traced back to the earliest days of the republic, when a nation was created committed to liberty yet resting, to a considerable extent, on slavery. Slavery helped to shape the identity, the sense of self, of all Americans, giving nationhood from the outset a powerful exclusionary dimension. It made the value of American citizenship, as Judith

Shklar has argued, rest to a considerable extent on its denial to others. Constituting the most impenetrable boundary of citizenship, slavery rendered blacks all but invisible to those imagining the American community. Slaves, as the nation's first attorney general, Edmund Randolph, wrote, were "not . . . constituent members of our society," and the language of liberty and citizenship did not apply to them. When the era's master mythmaker, Hector St. John Crèvecoeur, posed the famous question "What then is the American, the new man?" he answered: "a mixture of English, Scotch, Irish, French, Dutch, Germans, and Swedes. . . . He is either a European, or the descendant of a European." This at a time when fully one-fifth of the population (the highest proportion in our history) consisted of Africans and their descendants.

What of those within the "circle of we"? Nowhere does the original Constitution define who in fact are citizens of the United States, or what privileges and immunities they enjoy. Rather, the individual states were to determine the boundaries of citizenship and citizens' legal rights. The Constitution does, however, empower Congress to create a uniform system of naturalization, and the Naturalization Law of 1790 offered the first legislative definition of American nationality. With no debate, Congress restricted the process of becoming a citizen to "free white persons." This limitation lasted a long time. For eighty years, only white immigrants could become naturalized citizens. Blacks were added in 1870, but not until the 1940s did persons of Asian origin become eligible. Only in the last quarter of the nineteenth century were groups of whites barred from entering the country and becoming citizens. Beginning with prostitutes, convicted felons, lunatics, polygamists, and persons likely to become a "public charge," the list of excluded classes would be expanded in the twentieth century to include, among others, anarchists, communists, and the illiterate. But for the first century of the republic, virtually the only white persons in the entire world ineligible to claim American citizenship were those unwilling to renounce hereditary titles of nobility, as required in an act of 1795. For whites, here was as voluntarist a definition of nationality as could be imagined.

The two groups excluded from naturalization—European aristocrats and nonwhites—had more in common than might appear at first glance. Both were viewed as deficient in the qualities essential for republican citizenship, particularly the capacity for self-control, rational forethought, and devotion to the larger community. These were the characteristics that Jefferson, in his famous comparison of the races in *Notes on the State of Virginia*, claimed blacks lacked, partly due to natural incapacity and partly because the bitter experience of slavery had (quite understandably, he felt) rendered them disloyal to the nation. Like current writers, Jefferson was obsessed with the connection between heredity and environment, race and intelligence; unlike them, he offered tentative, not "scientific" conclusions. Jefferson believed black Americans should eventually enjoy the natural rights enumerated in the Declaration, but in Africa or the Caribbean, not in the United States. America should have a homogeneous citizenry whose common experiences, values, and innate capacities made it possible to realize the idea of the public good.

Blacks formed no part of the imagined community of Jefferson's republic. And whether free or slave, their status became increasingly anomalous as political democracy (for white men) expanded in the nineteenth century. Indeed, in a country that lacked more traditional bases of nationality—

long-established physical boundaries, a powerful and menacing neighbor, historic ethnic, religious, and cultural unity—America's democratic political institutions themselves came to define the nation. Increasingly, the right to vote became the emblem of citizenship—if not in law (since suffrage was still a privilege rather than a right, subject to regulation by the individual states), then in common usage and understanding. Noah Webster's *American Dictionary* noted that the term *citizen* had, by the 1820s, become synonymous with the right to vote.

Various groups of Americans, of course, stood outside this boundary. Free women were certainly members of the imagined community called the nation; indeed, according to the prevailing ideology of separate spheres, they played an indispensable role in the training of future citizens. The common law subsumed women within the legal status of their husbands. But courts generally (although not always) held that married women had a civic status of their own. They could be naturalized if immigrating from abroad, and except for a fifteen-year period beginning in 1907, a native-born American woman did not lose her nationality by marrying a foreigner. In both law and social reality, however, women lacked the essential qualification of political participation—the opportunity for autonomy based on ownership of property or control of one's own labor. Women were also widely believed (by men) to be naturally submissive, by definition unfit for citizenship.

If women occupied a position of subordinate citizenship, nonwhites were increasingly excluded from the imagined community altogether. Slaves, of course, were by definition outside the "circle of we," and even in the North, democracy for whites, including immigrants from abroad, expanded hand in hand with deterioration in the status of blacks. In 1821, the same New York Constitutional Convention that removed property requirements for white voters raised the qualification for blacks to $250—a sum beyond the reach of nearly all the state's black residents. In effect, race had replaced class as the principal criterion of citizenship. Chief Justice Roger B. Taney gave legitimacy to this position in the *Dred Scott* decision of 1857, which ruled that no black person could be a citizen of the United States.

The relationship between inclusion and exclusion was symbiotic, not contradictory. Even as Americans' rhetoric grew ever more egalitarian, a fully developed racist ideology gained broad acceptance as the explanation for the boundaries of nationality. As in the case of women, nature itself—inborn incapacity rather than human contrivance—explained the exclusion of nonwhites. Of course, as John Stuart Mill once asked, "Was there ever any domination which did not appear natural to those who possessed it?" Yet Mill himself argued in his great work, *On Liberty*, that the right to self-government applied "only to human beings in the maturity of their faculties." Entire "races" lacked the capacity for rational action essential to democratic citizenship.

Mill's view was widely shared in the United States. Perhaps this was inevitable in a nation whose economic growth depended in large measure on the labor of black slaves and whose territorial expansion involved the dispossession of one nonwhite people, the Indians, and the conquest of the lands inhabited by another deemed nonwhite, the Mexicans. Indeed, westward expansion created a sense, among white Americans, of land ownership as an entitlement of citizenship. Yet the West, imagined and experienced by white laborers as a land of economic independence, simultaneously harbored not only slavery but indentured Indian labor, Mexican-American peonage, and work under long-term contracts for Chinese immigrants. Free labor was an entitlement of whites alone. The rhetoric of racial exclusion suffused the political language. "I believe this government was made on the white basis," said Stephen A. Douglas in his debates with Lincoln. "I believe it was made by white men for the benefit of white men and their posterity for ever, and I am in favor of confining citizenship to white men . . . instead of conferring it upon negroes, Indians, and other inferior races." Even as this focus on "race" (in the nineteenth century an amorphous category amalgamating ideas about culture, history, religion, and color) helped to solidify a sense of national identity among the diverse groups of European origin that made up the free population, it drew ever more tightly the lines of exclusion of America's imagined community.

Yet if slavery spawned a racialized definition of American nationality, the struggle for abolition gave rise to its opposite, a purely civic version of citizenship. The antislavery crusade insisted on the "Americanness" of slaves and free blacks and repudiated not only slavery but the racial boundaries that confined free blacks to second-class status. Abolitionists pioneered the idea of a national citizenship whose members enjoyed equality before the law protected by a beneficent national state. Although far less egalitarian, Republicans in the 1850s also insisted that America's professed creed was broad enough to encompass all mankind. Speaking of European immigrants, Abraham Lincoln noted that their membership in the American community derived neither from "blood" nor ancestral connection with the revolution but rather from the "moral sentiment" of universal equality and liberty. Lincoln explicitly rejected Douglas's race-based definition of liberty, insisting that the rights enumerated in the Declaration of Independence applied to all peoples.

Thus, the crisis of the Union, among other things, was a crisis of the meaning of American nationhood, and the Civil War a crucial moment that redefined the boundaries of citizenship. Mobilization for warfare often produces an emphasis on national unity, and throughout our history wars have galvanized disempowered citizens to lay claim to their rights. Women and American Indians received the right to vote in the aftermath of World War I; eighteen-year-olds did so during the Vietnam War. The Civil War not only consolidated national loyalties but created the modern American nation-state. Inevitably, it propelled the question "Who is an American?" to the forefront of public discussion. "It is a singular fact," Wendell Phillips wrote in 1866, "that, unlike all other nations, this nation has yet a question as to what makes or constitutes a citizen." The war produced the first formal delineation of American citizenship, a vast expansion of citizen's rights, and a repudiation of the idea that these rights attached to persons in their capacity as members of certain ethnic or racial groups rather than as members of an undifferentiated American people.

A new concept of Americanism emerged from the Civil War. The first statutory definition of American citizenship, the Civil Rights Act of 1866, declared all persons born in the United States (except Indians) national citizens and spelled out rights they were to enjoy equally without regard to race—the ability, essentially, to compete in the marketplace, own property, and receive equal treatment before the law. The Fourteenth Amendment placed in the Constitution the definition of

citizenship as birth on American soil or naturalization and prohibited states from abridging any citizens' "privileges and immunities" or denying them "equal protection of the law." This
broad language opened the door for future Congresses and the
federal courts to breathe substantive meaning into the guarantee of legal equality, a process that has occupied the courts for
much of the last century. Then, the Fifteenth Amendment
barred the states from making race a qualification for voting.

Because what Republican leader Carl Schurz called "the
great Constitutional revolution" of Reconstruction represented
so striking a departure from the previous traditions of American law, it aroused bitter opposition. "We are not of the same
race," declared Indiana senator Thomas Hendricks, "we are
so different that we ought not to compose one political
community."

Reconstruction Republicans rejected this reasoning, but
their universalism too had its limits. In his remarkable "Com-
posite Nation" speech of 1869, Frederick Douglass condemned
prejudice against immigrants from China, insisting that America's destiny was to serve as an asylum for people "gathered
here from all corners of the globe by a common aspiration for
national liberty." Any form of exclusion, he insisted, contradicted the essence of democracy. A year later Charles Sumner,
the Senate's leading Radical Republican, moved to strike the
word *white* from naturalization requirements. Senators from
the western states objected vociferously. They were willing to
admit blacks to citizenship but not Asians. At their insistence,
the racial boundaries of nationality were widened but not
eliminated.

Nor did Reconstruction policymakers make any effort to expand the definition of citizenship rights to incorporate women.

Reconstruction, declared Universalist minister and suffrage leader Olympia Brown, offered the opportunity to "bury the black man and the woman in the citizen." Yet Republicans—including many former slaves—saw emancipation as restoring to blacks the natural right to family life, in which men would take their place as heads of the household and women theirs in the domestic sphere from which slavery had unnaturally removed them. Indeed, when women tried to employ the Fourteenth Amendment's expanded definition of citizenship to press their own rights, they found the courts unreceptive. Citizenship, declared Chief Justice Morrison Waite, was compatible with disenfranchisement; it meant "membership of a nation and nothing more." The Court's argument regarding women was a harbinger of a more general narrowing of the definition of citizenship. With the end of Reconstruction, the egalitarian impulse faded from national life, and the imagined community was reimagined once again.

The "failure" of Reconstruction strongly reinforced the racialist thinking that reemerged to dominate American culture in the late nineteenth century, fueling the conviction that nonwhites were unfit for self-government. "A black skin," Columbia University political scientist John W. Burgess would write at the turn of the century, "means membership in a race of men which has never of itself succeeded in subjecting passion to reason, and has never, therefore, created any civilization of any kind." The retreat from the postwar ideal of color-blind citizenship was also reflected in the resurgence of an Anglo-Saxonism that united patriotism, xenophobia, and an ethnocultural definition of nationhood in a renewed rhetoric of racial exclusiveness. America's triumphant entry onto the world stage as an imperial power in the Spanish-American War of 1898 tied nationalism more and more closely to notions of Anglo-Saxon superiority, displacing in part the earlier identification of the United States with democratic political institutions (or defining those institutions in a more and more explicitly racial manner). In the Progressive era, citizenship's boundaries narrowed even as its substance expanded. As the "labor question" came to dominate public life, so too did the idea that citizenship must have an economic content. Progressive leaders like Louis Brandeis and Theodore Roosevelt insisted that in an age of corporate capitalism, the "essentials of American citizenship" had come to include "freedom in things industrial," such as the right to education, "some degree of financial independence," and "social insurance" as a guarantee against unemployment and poverty. Here was a social definition of citizenship whose influence would extend to the New Deal and beyond. But the progressives also envisioned a strong state as an agency of Americanization, which would forge a unified community in the face of the demographic changes overtaking the society, dissolving ethnic identities and making the new immigrants full members of the nation. Like today's proponents of a common culture and common values, the progressives, in fact, were amazingly ambiguous when it came to the actual content of Americanism. One searches their speeches in vain for any precise definition of American values, apart from belief in democracy and loyalty to this nation rather than to an immigrant's land of origins.

The most vocal advocates of Americanism continued to adhere to a racialized definition. In the idea of an "American standard of living," the American Federation of Labor popularized an identification of high wages with national identity, while simultaneously insisting that Asians, blacks, and new immigrants from Europe were by nature willing to work for "slave wages" and thus were not truly American. Other self-proclaimed defenders of America's racial and cultural heritage warned of the danger posed by "lower races"—a term that included immigrants from southern and eastern Europe. This racialist language inherited from the nineteenth century acquired a pseudoscientific underpinning in the newly invented concept of IQ and in birth-rate statistics "demonstrating" that the less able were in danger of overrunning the superior races and undermining the nation's genetic purity. (Similar calculations by today's opponents of nonwhite immigration say nothing that cannot be found in Madison Grant's *Passing of the Great Race* eight decades ago. The only difference is that today's nativists romanticize the immigrants of the Progressive era as self-reliant individuals who, unlike modern counterparts, did not rely on public assistance or commit violent crimes. This portrait of turn-of-the-century immigrants as self-reliant and law-abiding would have amazed Americanizers of those days, who leveled against Italians, Jews, and Poles the very same charges of inferior intelligence, dependence on public assistance, and propensity to criminality wielded today against Haitians, Mexicans, and others.)

The idea that the new immigrants were representatives of distinct races unfit for democratic citizenship fueled renewed efforts to narrow the boundaries of nationhood. Congress had already prohibited the further entry of immigrants from China. In 1921 and 1924, in a fundamental break with the tradition of open entry for whites except for specifically designated classes of undesirables, it imposed the first sharp numerical limits on European immigration, establishing a nationality quota system that sought to ensure that new immigrants would never outnumber descendants of the old. The same intellectual linkage of race, intelligence, and Americanism inspired laws to reduce the number of "feebleminded" through sterilization, a practice upheld in 1927 by the Supreme Court as a way of improving the quality of the American population. At this time too, a concerted effort was made to revise school curricula to make the teaching of American history more patriotic.

By the 1920s, with black disenfranchisement in the South, the exclusion of Asians from entering the country, the repudiation of the idea of "industrial democracy" in favor of industry's American Plan, and the broad segmentation of immigration and labor markets along racial, ethnic, and gender lines, the boundaries and substantive content of American citizenship had again been severely curtailed. But as always, these remained points of intense social conflict. Progressivism may have given impetus to a homogenized Americanism, but progressives such as Horace Kallen and Randolph Bourne reinvigorated the civic definition of nationality and insisted that democracy thrived on group difference, not artificial homogeneity. America, wrote Bourne, was a "federation of cultures," not an Anglo-Saxon preserve.

In some respects, cultural pluralism (a term coined by Kallen in 1924) was as vague an idea as the demand for adherence to "American values"—it often seemed to amount to little more than belief in democracy and tolerance of group difference. These pluralists, moreover, had remarkably little to say about the place of nonwhites in American society. But they effectively challenged the idea that the new immigrants from southern and eastern Europe were unfit to become citizens, or could do so only by abandoning their traditions in favor of Anglo-Saxon ways. Meanwhile, anthropologists Franz Boas,

Alfred Kroeber, and Ruth Benedict offered intellectual legitimacy to the idea that differences among social groups arose
from history and experience, not from biology, and challenged
the prevailing notion that societies or races inhabited a fixed
spectrum running from "primitive" to "civilized."

Anthropologies, however, do not generally shape public policy. Despite broad acceptance among intellectuals, the celebration of diversity remained a minority point of view until World
War II, when it suddenly emerged as the official definition of
American nationhood. The way, to be sure, had already been
paved during the New Deal by the resurgent union movement
and the broad left-wing culture of the Popular Front era. The
CIO mobilized ethnically divided industrial workers into a self-
conscious class with a broad social definition of citizenship and
an emphasis on pluralism and inclusiveness as the American
way. Meanwhile left-wing artists and intellectuals advanced a
new conception of America as a multiethnic, pluralist nation
(including even blacks). By 1940, the idea that the country's
strength lay in diversity and tolerance had been so widely disseminated that Earl Robinson's "Ballad for Americans," a quin-
tessential expression of the pluralist Popular Front culture, was
sung at the Republican party's national convention.

Only the mobilization for World War II and the confrontation with Nazism, however, purged Americanism of the language of race. No longer identified as members of distinct
"races," Italians, Poles, Jews, and the other new immigrants
became hyphenated ethnics, or to put it another way, they
merged into a general category of white Americans. Meanwhile, for the first time since Reconstruction, the status of blacks
reemerged as a concern of national policy, partly because of
the demands of blacks themselves and partly because of the

contradiction between the nation's racial system and its claim to be fighting a global battle for democracy and equality against demonic theories of a master race. The war even led to the inclusion of Chinese in the ranks of those eligible for naturalized citizenship (although the annual quota of 105 did not suggest a desire for large-scale immigration from Asia). As the ethnic understanding of Americanism was discredited, President Roosevelt explicitly committed the nation to the civic definition. To be an American, he insisted, had always been a "matter of mind and heart" and "never was a matter of race or ancestry"—a statement more attuned to mobilizing support for the war than to accurately describing the American past. The onset of the cold war reinforced this official definition of the United States as a diverse nation committed to a creed of equality, liberty, and democracy and open to all who desired freedom.

The rise of the civil rights movement further invigorated the civic, inclusionary definition of American nationality. The movement reclaimed the color-blind ideals of the Reconstruction era, erased the second-class legal status of black citizens, and, not coincidentally, inspired the elimination of the nationality quota system for immigration. Only time will tell whether the widespread acceptance of civic nationalism was a permanent change in American life or the product of specific circumstances, some of which—the cold war, an expanding economy capable of absorbing immigrants, and a broad national commitment to eradicating racial inequality—are already fading into history.

Historians, Eric Hobsbawm writes in his recent chronicle of the twentieth century, are the "professional remembrancers of what their fellow citizens wish to forget." Americans often "forget" that our history is not a Whiggish progress toward greater and greater freedom and equality but a far more complex story in which gains are made and lost, rights are expanded and sometimes revoked, and ideas long since discredited rise like ghosts to haunt later generations. If our history teaches anything, it is that the question "Who is an American?" has never had a fixed or simple answer. It seems safe to predict that in the twenty-first century, the boundaries of our imagined community will continue to be a source of political conflict and social struggle.

EIGHT

BLACKS AND
THE U.S. CONSTITUTION

❧

In 1989, I was asked to deliver the Herbert Gutman Memorial Lecture at the City University of New York, named for a close friend and one of his generation's most innovative historians. This was shortly after historical understandings of the Reconstruction era and the Fourteenth Amendment had suddenly emerged as a political issue—both in contentious Senate hearings on President Reagan's nomination of Robert Bork to the Supreme Court, and in Attorney General Edwin Meese's insistence that the Court should repudiate the tradition, based on that amendment, of requiring the states to abide by the guarantees of individual liberties set forth in the Constitution's Bill of Rights.

I decided to speak on the long, complex constitutional history of African-Americans. The lecture concluded with a critique of recent Supreme Court decisions on racial issues and of the historical assumptions and, to my mind, misconceptions adhered to by the Court's majority.

Since this essay was written, the Court's basic approach to civil rights issues and its interpretation of the Fourteenth Amendment have remained intact (despite changes in its membership). Over the past decade, the justices have continued to employ the amendment's equal protection clause primarily to support white plaintiffs who claim to be suffering "reverse discrimination" from affirmative action programs. The Court still appears to view "racial classifications," not inequality, as the root of the country's race problems. It continues to demand proof of discriminatory intent before being willing to support black plaintiffs challenging the actions of public officials or private employers rather than demanding explanations of why policies have a discriminatory impact.

On the basis of these assumptions and positions, it has in recent years invalidated affirmative action policies, made it easier for school districts to free themselves from judicial desegregation orders, and allowed local authorities to alter governmental procedures so as to reduce the power of black elected officials.

The Court has also continued its resurrection of state-centered federalism, shielding states, for example, from antidiscrimination lawsuits authorized by federal law. Thus far, the federalism decisions have centered on claims of discrimination by women and persons with disabilities, rather than issues relating to race, but they appear to lay the groundwork for a further retreat from the enforcement of civil rights more generally.

Underlying the Court's ongoing abandonment of the role of active advocate for the rights of disadvantaged Americans remains a cramped and ahistorical understanding of the Fourteenth Amendment and Reconstruction.

On July 4, 1854, the abolitionist William Lloyd Garrison addressed a large Independence Day gathering at Framingham, Massachusetts. One month earlier a federal tribunal in Boston had ordered Anthony Burns, a fugitive from slavery, returned to his Virginia owner. Garrison had long since established a reputation for outraging respectable opinion by his militant condemnation of slavery and its defenders, North and South. But on this day, he outdid himself. First, he burned a copy of the Fugitive Slave Law of 1850, under which Burns had been returned to bondage. Then he burned the court decision. Finally, he held aloft "the parent of all the other atrocities"—the Constitution. Calling it "a covenant with death, an agreement with hell," Garrison set it on fire.

Garrison, of course, was neither the first nor the last American to believe that the Constitution's provisions regarding slavery fatally undermined its claim to "establish justice" and promote the "general welfare." During the recent commemoration of the Constitution's bicentennial, Supreme Court Justice Thurgood Marshall pointedly reminded the country of those excluded from the founders' definition of human rights. Marshall, one suspects, was reacting not simply to the unrelentingly celebratory nature of the occasion but to the charge by Attorney General Edwin Meese, rejected Supreme Court nominee Robert Bork, and other conservatives that federal judges should confine themselves to implementing the "original intent" of the Constitution's framers. Not all Americans, Marshall suggested, consider that intent entirely benign.

In an age of semiotics and deconstruction, not to mention intense debate among historians about the prevailing ideas of the revolutionary era, there is something refreshingly naïve, almost quaint, in the idea that any text, including the Constitution, possesses a single, easily ascertainable, objective meaning. Of course, the call for a jurisprudence of "original intent" is less a carefully thought-out intellectual stance than a political rallying cry, a justification for the undoing of modern Supreme Court decisions that have broadened the definition of constitutional rights, especially for black Americans. Whether the Supreme Court *should* be bound by the "original intent" of the Constitutional text is a political, not a historical, question. But the current debate over originalism does have the virtue of directing our attention to the two interrelated issues with which this essay is concerned—the history of constitutional law and Supreme Court decisions concerning African-Americans, and how differing understandings of that history continue to play a central part in the debate over civil rights. Rather than attempting the impossible task of surveying all of American history, I will focus on three key moments—the Constitutional Convention itself, the rewriting of the Constitution during Reconstruction, and the most recent rulings of Supreme Court.

When the struggle for independence began, slavery was already an old institution in America. For well over a century, slaves had tilled the tobacco fields of Virginia and Maryland; for nearly as long they had labored on the rice plantations of coastal South Carolina. Slaves also worked on small farms in parts of the North and in many artisan shops in cities like New York and Philadelphia. Taking the nation as a whole, one American in five was a black slave in 1776.

Among both blacks and whites, the Revolution inspired widespread hopes that slavery might be removed from American life. With the British offering freedom to slaves who joined the royal cause, tens of thousands fled their owners and gained their liberty. Thousands of others escaped bondage by enlisting in the Continental Army. During the 1780s, a considerable number of Southern slaveholders, especially in Virginia and Maryland, voluntarily emancipated their slaves. By the early nineteenth century, every state from Pennsylvania north to New Hampshire had taken steps to abolish slavery. Nonetheless, the stark fact is that there were considerably more slaves at the end of the revolutionary era than at the beginning. The first national census, in 1790, revealed that the half-million slave population of 1776 had grown to some 700,000.

American statesmen, including slaveholders like Washington and Jefferson, were fully aware that slavery blatantly violated the Revolution's professed ideals. But to call slavery an ambiguity or even a contradiction in the minds of the founders is to fail to confront the institution's centrality in late-eighteenth-century America and the strength of the barriers to abolition. Slavery was already the foundation of social and economic life in the Southern states. Racism was well entrenched nationwide. And in an era that saw ownership of property as the basis of individual freedom, the sanctity of property rights formed a powerful bulwark of slavery. This entrenchment was demonstrated not only by the failure of abolition in the South but by its slowness in the North, where slavery was peripheral to the economy. In New York, for example, the emancipation law of 1799 freed no living slave; it merely provided for the liberty of any child born to a slave mother, and only after he or she had served the mother's master until adulthood as compensation for the owner's future loss of property rights.

The fifty-five men who gathered at the Constitutional Convention in 1787 included numerous slaveholders, as well as some dedicated abolitionists. As James Madison recorded, in many of the debates, "the institution of slavery and its consequences formed the line of discrimination." Although their implications are often misunderstood, the Constitution's key provisions regarding slavery are easily summarized. First, Congress was prohibited from abolishing the importation of slaves into the country for twenty years. Second, the states were required to return to their owners all fugitives from bondage. Third, in determining each state's representation in the House of Representatives and its electoral votes for President, three-fifths of the slaves would be counted along with the free population. It should be noted that in deference to the sensibilities of some delegates, the words *slave* and *slavery* did not appear in the original Constitution—instead, such terms as "other persons" and persons "held to service or labour" were used. As Luther Martin, a Maryland attorney who attended the Constitutional Convention but bitterly opposed ratification, wrote, his fellow delegates "anxiously sought to avoid the admission of expressions which might be odious in the ears of Americans." But, he went on, they were "willing to admit into their system those *things* which the *expressions* signified."

Clearly the Constitution's slavery clauses were compromises, efforts to find a middle ground between the institution's critics and defenders. But the Southern states had the advantage that they would not agree to a Constitution that threatened slavery, while abolition was a minor concern to most Northerners. Thus, it should not be surprising that taken together, these clauses strengthened the institution of slavery and left it even more deeply embedded in American life and politics. The slave trade clause allowed a commerce condemned by civilized society, and against which laws had been passed by the Continental Congress and most of the states, to continue into the nineteenth century. Partly to replace slaves who had escaped to the British and partly because of the expansion of cotton production after the invention of the cotton gin in 1793, South Carolina and Georgia took advantage of the twenty-year hiatus before abolition of the trade to import some forty thousand additional Africans—about ten percent of all slaves brought to British North America from colonial times to 1808. The fugitive slave clause accorded slave laws "extraterritoriality"—that is, the condition of bondage adhered to a person even if he or she escaped to a jurisdiction where slavery had been abolished. It made all the states, and the federal government, complicitous in maintaining the institution's stability. The three-fifths clause allowed the white South to exercise far greater power in national affairs than its numbers warranted. It produced, said Luther Martin, "the absurdity of increasing the power of a State in making laws for free men in proportion as that State violated the rights of freedom." Partly as a result, of the first sixteen presidential elections between 1788 and 1848, all but four placed a Southern slaveholder in the White House. It is worth noting that the much-maligned Articles of Confederation, which the Constitution replaced, had no three-fifths clause magnifying Southern political power, and no fugitive slave clause (although it did require states to surrender persons charged with "treason, felony, or other high misdemeanor"). Whatever its other merits, the Constitution represented a step backward when it came to slavery.

The government's federal structure under the Constitution, moreover, insulated slavery from outside interference. Many of the founders, of course, had become disgusted with the weakness of the central government under the Articles of Confederation and were obsessed with the danger of what Madison called "democratic despotism" in the states, reflected in laws suspending the collection of debts and making paper money legal tender. They hoped the Constitutional Convention would create a stronger national government able to act as a brake on the turbulence and unpredictability of state politics. Madison, indeed, unsuccessfully proposed to give Congress the authority to overturn state laws—an idea that would have had immense, if unintended, implications for slavery. But while the Constitution strengthened national authority, it did not create a centralized national state. In 1816, the federal government employed fewer than five thousand persons, two-thirds of them in the post office, and such crucial concerns of government as taxation, education, and the definition and protection of citizen's rights were left to state and local authorities. The Bill of Rights, which protected basic liberties against infringement by the national government but not the states, indicated that most Americans still believed centralized government posed the greatest threat to their liberties.

"For all that is contained in this constitution," an anonymous Pennsylvania pamphleteer noted in 1787, "this country may remain degraded by this impious custom till the end of time." This indisputable fact posed a severe challenge for the antislavery movement that emerged in the nineteenth century. Some abolitionists, like Garrison, branded the Constitution proslavery and called for its abrogation. A few, such as Lysander Spooner, developed an elaborate if unpersuasive argument to show that under the Constitution, slavery was in fact illegal. Spooner relied on the Fifth Amendment, which barred the federal government from depriving any person of life, liberty, or property without due process of law. Ultimately, however, his position rested on the supremacy of natural rights to the Constitution. Many proponents of antislavery politics, like Salmon P. Chase and Abraham Lincoln, took a middle view, insisting that the founding fathers had hoped for the institution's "ultimate extinction" and had done nothing to prevent abolition by the individual states. The Constitution, Chase insisted, created no federal responsibility for slavery, a position difficult to reconcile with the fugitive slave clause. The fact that the Constitution rendered the national government powerless to interfere directly with slavery did much to shape subsequent antislavery politics, steering it toward a focus on preventing slavery's expansion into the territories, where Congress did possess the authority to act, and not on ending slavery in the states where it actually existed.

Frederick Douglass, who originally held the Garrisonian view of a proslavery Constitution, subsequently changed his mind, although his tortuous logic suggests that his motivation lay in political expediency rather than deep conviction. The founders' original intent, Douglass argued, was proslavery, but the text itself did not prohibit federal action against bondage. Hence the Garrisonians were wrong to oppose political involvement by abolitionists. Douglass held to this position throughout the 1850s, even as a more nationalistic group of black abolitionists turned the idea of a proslavery Constitution into an argument for emigration from the United States. Far from being a "foreign element" in American life or some kind of aberration, insisted H. Ford Douglass, slavery had received the sanction of the founding fathers, and blacks could never secure equality in America.

Did blacks form part of the "We the People" who created the Constitution? Or were they simply "other persons" outside the political nation? For most of the antebellum period, the power to define citizenship rights rested with the states. And despite their differences regarding the national Constitution, abolitionists, white and black, worked tirelessly to secure legal recognition of Northern blacks' equality before the law. They faced, to say the least, an uphill struggle. The North's tiny black community, amounting to only one percent of the region's population on the eve of the Civil War, was subjected to discrimination in every phase of its life. Despite the spread of antislavery sentiment, Northern racism seemed to deepen as the century progressed. By 1860, five Northern states had prohibited all blacks from entering their territory. Democracy itself increasingly took on a racial definition. Between 1800 and 1860, every free state but Maine that entered the Union, beginning with Ohio in 1803, restricted voting to white males. Among older states, even as property qualifications for whites faded, blacks found their political rights more and more restricted. Pennsylvania, home of an articulate, economically successful black community in Philadelphia, eliminated black voting entirely in 1837.

This melancholy history forms the background for the most famous pre–Civil War Supreme Court pronouncement relating to blacks' rights under the Constitution, the *Dred Scott* decision. In effect, Chief Justice Roger B. Taney turned the arguments of antislavery constitutionalists on their head. Far from securing the freedom of the slaves by its protection of individual liberty, the Fifth Amendment, by its guarantee of property rights, prevented Congress from barring slavery's extension into any territory. Judge Bork, in his new book *The Tempting of America*, calls this the "worst constitutional decision of the nineteenth century." (The twentieth century's "worst," it will surprise no one to learn, was *Roe v. Wade*, legalizing abortion.) But Bork, interestingly enough, says nothing about Taney's attempt to explore the founders' original intent or his famous conclusion that under the Constitution, no black person could be a citizen of the United States. The Court, Taney argued, must be guided by the racial views of the revolutionary generation, and blacks "were at that time considered as a subordinate and inferior class of beings, who had been subjugated by the dominant race, and whether emancipated or not, yet remained subject to their authority. . . . They had no rights which the white man was bound to respect." A state could accord blacks rights if it wished, but the Constitution did not require other states to accord them, as it did for whites, the "privileges and immunities" of citizens. To the historian, Taney's interpretation of the founders' intentions regarding blacks is certainly plausible. *Dred Scott* may have been morally reprehensible, but it was good constitutional law—if, that is, good constitutional law means continually reenacting the principles and prejudices of the founding fathers.

What swept *Dred Scott* into the dustbin of history, of course, was not a reinterpretation of the founders' views but the greatest cataclysm in our history. The Civil War and Reconstruction produced not simply three amendments but a fundamentally new Constitution. The Thirteenth, Fourteenth, and Fifteenth Amendments abolished slavery, established a national citizenship whose rights, enforced by the federal government, were to be enjoyed equally by all Americans, and protected the right to vote of black men. These measures altered the definition of American citizenship, transformed the federal system, and engrafted into the Constitution a principle of racial equality entirely unprecedented in both jurisprudence and political reality before 1860.

Two developments during the Civil War were responsible for placing the issue of black citizenship on the national agenda. One was the process of emancipation itself and especially the massive enrollment of blacks into the Union armed forces. The "logical result" of black military service, one senator observed in 1864, was that "the black man is henceforth to assume a new status among us." The second was a profound alteration in the nature of American government. The mobilization of the North's resources for modern war created what one Republican called "a new government," with greatly expanded powers and responsibilities. And the war inspired a broad nationalism, embraced above all by antislavery reformers, black and white, and Radical Republicans in Congress. With emancipation, these men and women believed, the federal government had become not a threat to individual liberty but the "custodian of freedom."

The amendments and civil rights laws reflected the intersection of these two products of the Civil War era—the newly empowered national state and the idea of a national citizenship enjoying equality before the law. The Thirteenth Amendment, which became part of the Constitution in 1865, irrevocably abolished slavery (for the first time given its actual name in the Constitution rather than being mentioned via circumlocution) and empowered Congress to enforce emancipation with "appropriate legislation." The amendment raised a question fundamental to political and social debate during Reconstruction: the definition of freedom. "What is freedom?" asked Congressman James A. Garfield. "Is it the bare privilege of not being chained? . . . If this is all, then freedom is a bitter mockery, a cruel delusion." The former slaves understood freedom to mean personal autonomy, economic independence, and equal rights as citizens. Congressional Republicans, under the impact of the continuing political crisis of Reconstruction, moved first toward equality before the law and equal rights for blacks as free laborers in the economic marketplace, then to a broader vision of equal political participation, and finally to equal access to public accommodations.

This is not the occasion to trace the tangled history of social conflict and constitutional change during Reconstruction. Since recent debate has focused on the Civil Rights Act of 1866 and the Fourteenth Amendment, I will confine myself today to these. The Civil Rights Act defined all persons born in the United States (except Indians) as national citizens, and it spelled out rights they were to enjoy without regard to race— including making contracts, bringing lawsuits, owning property, and receiving equal treatment before the courts and by government officials. No action by a state, or local custom, could deprive an individual of these basic rights; if it did, state officials would be held accountable in federal court.

At the most basic level, the Civil Rights Act aimed to overturn the *Dred Scott* decision and to invalidate the South's recently enacted Black Codes, which severely limited the freedmen's economic prospects and standing before the law. The first statutory definition of freedom under the Thirteenth Amendment, the act's listing of specific rights focused on those central to the Republicans' free labor ideology—the rights to choose one's employment, to enforce payment of wages, and to compete on equal terms for advancement in the economic marketplace. But beyond these, Republicans also rejected the entire idea of legal distinctions among citizens based on race, and the act invalidated many discriminatory laws on the Northern statute book as well as the Southern. The underlying assumption—that the federal government possessed the power to define and protect citizens' rights—was a striking departure in American law. Indeed, declared President Andrew Johnson, who vetoed the bill only to see it reenacted by Congress, federal protection of blacks' civil rights and the broad conception of national power that lay behind it violated "all our experience as a people." Moreover, Johnson went on, clothing blacks with the privileges of citizenship discriminated against whites—"the distinction of race and color is by the bill made to operate in favor of the colored and against the white race."

Unlike the Civil Rights Act, which listed specific rights no state could violate, the Fourteenth Amendment, approved by Congress in June 1866, sought to establish equality among citizens in general language. Its heart was the first section, which prohibited the states from abridging citizens' "privileges and immunities," depriving any person of life, liberty, or property without "due process of law," or denying "equal protection of the laws." Because of its broad, elusive wording, the amendment's meaning has probably inspired more disagreement than any other clause of the Constitution. Proponents of "original intent" castigate the modern Supreme Court for "judicial activisim" in interpreting its provisions. Attorney General Meese criticized the Court for adopting the legal doctrine known as "incorporation," which holds that the amendment requires the states to respect the prohibitions on the abuse of power originally applied to the federal government by the Bill of Rights.

Judge Bork believes the amendment aimed only to protect blacks against explicitly discriminatory state and local laws—any other use is an example of judges substituting their views for those of the framers. Meese, Bork, and others are reluctant to take the amendment at face value, as a statement of general principle rather than an enactment of specific legislative purposes, because they fear this would leave too much leeway for judicial interpretation. They see the Fourteenth Amendment as a minor adjustment to the Constitution, not a change in its basic structure. Their cramped reading reminds me of a recent Herblock cartoon depicting Justices Rehnquist, Scalia, and other worthies, with the caption "They revere the Constitution, it's just some of the Amendments they don't like."

It is most ironic that proponents of "original intent," a principle that explicitly appeals to history to guide judicial rulings, apparently know nothing of the actual history of Reconstruction. For if anything is clear from the historical record, it is that Congress chose broad, indeterminate language precisely to allow leeway for interpreting and implementing the amendment, and that it envisioned an active role for the federal judiciary in enforcement. It is certainly true that Congress did not expect the courts to perpetually frustrate the will of state legislatures. But to leave it at this ignores an obvious but often-neglected point: the men who made the Fourteenth Amendment expected the states to abide by it. Indeed, in the now-forgotten third section, they moved to limit political power in the South to genuine supporters of the Union who, they believed, would respect the amendment's provisions, rending national enforcement unnecessary. Nobody anticipated that nearly a century of nullification would follow Reconstruction. But if national action to protect citizens' rights did become necessary, Congress placed the burden on Congress (specifically empowered by each of the era's amendments to enforce its provisions) and the federal courts, whose jurisdiction Congress vastly expanded during Reconstruction. In the absence of a standing army, national police force, or permanent Freedman's Bureau, this seemed the best means of guaranteeing the basic rights of American citizens against violations by the states. Thus, the judicial activism of the past generation is really in keeping with the intentions of the amendment's framers.

The redefinition of federalism and the establishment of a national principle of equality before the law worked a profound transformation in blacks' political outlook. Before 1860, most blacks had feared federal power, since the government at Washington seemed to be controlled by the Slave Power. Indeed, some Northern states in effect nullified the national fugitive slave law before the Civil War. But with emancipation and equal rights coming through unprecedented exercises of central authority, blacks fully embraced the nationalism of the Civil War era. Until Americans abandoned the idea of "the right of each State to control its own affairs," wrote Frederick Douglass, "no general assertion of human rights can be of any practical value." The states' inability to suppress political violence during Reconstruction reinforced this tendency to look to Washington for salvation. This identification with the national government, reinforced during the modern civil rights movement, remains to this day a major difference between black and white political traditions. Their distinct historical experience leads most blacks to fear unrestrained localism far more than an activist government at Washington, even while, as President Reagan demonstrated, talk of curbing national authority can still, two centuries after the American Revolution, galvanize white voters.

Even in the 1870s, in fact, the retreat from Reconstruction was fueled by a growing sense in the North that the federal government had grown too powerful, and that blacks were in danger of becoming, in the then-current phrase, "permanent wards" of the national state. And of course, in the abandonment of a national commitment to equal rights, the Supreme Court played a major and sorry role. Beginning with the *Slaughterhouse* cases in 1873, the Court progressively restricted the rights protected under the Fourteenth Amendment. In 1883 came the *Civil Rights* cases, invalidating a law prohibiting discrimination in public accommodations. Then, in 1896, *Plessy v. Ferguson* decreed that state-mandated racial segregation did not violate the equal protection clause. By the turn of the century, the states had been given carte blanche to nullify the Reconstruction amendments and civil rights laws. Not until our own time did a great mass movement and a socially conscious Supreme Court again breathe life into the racial egalitarianism and the broad view of citizens' rights that arose during Reconstruction.

To those who came of age during the era of the Warren Court, it is easy to forget that the Supreme Court, expected by the founding fathers to be the most conservative branch of the government, has amply fulfilled that role throughout most of our history. And today the Court appears poised to revert to its traditional function. If the civil rights movement of the 1950s and 1960s was often called the second Reconstruction, we now seem to have entered a second Redemption—as the restoration of white supremacy was called in the late-nineteenth-century South. Just as the Supreme Court slowly eviscerated the legal structure of the first Reconstruction, today's Court has begun to do the same for the second. A brief look at key decisions of the Court's last term will illustrate how.

Rather than voting rights, access to public accommodations, and segregation, the focal points of earlier civil rights litigation, the cases of 1989 turned on bread-and-butter issues—the right to hold a job and advance through promotion, and the responsibility of government and private employers to redress the past exclusion of blacks and other groups from large segments of the labor market. Unlike the celebrated *Bakke* case, which centered on admission to medical school, the 1989 plaintiffs included bank tellers, firemen, cannery workers, and construction contractors—representatives, as it were, of millions of working-class and lower-middle-class blacks. In the most publicized case, *Brenda Patterson v. McLean Credit Union,* a black teller who suffered racial harassment on the job sued for damages under the Civil Rights Act of 1866. The Court rejected her claim for punitive damages, contending that the law barred discrimination only at the moment of signing a contract; once Patterson was on the job, it did not apply. In another case, the Court ruled against a group of Filipino and Eskimo workers at an Alaska salmon cannery, who presented evidence that unskilled jobs were monopolized by nonwhites while the company confined skilled positions to whites. Such statistical disparities, the Court said, do not provide prima facie evidence of discriminatory intent. The Court also overturned a Richmond law reserving 30 percent of city construction contracts for minority businesses, and it allowed a group of white Birmingham firefighters to bring suit against a program previously adopted by the city fire department that set goals for the hiring and promotion of blacks. At the same time, the justices refused to allow a challenge to changes in AT&T's seniority system that adversely affected women employees, on the grounds that too much time had passed to initiate litigation.

Taken together, these decisions suggest some ominous conclusions about the Court's reading of the law and of American
history. Five judges (Rehnquist, White, O'Connor, Scalia, and
Kennedy) consistently voted to interpret civil rights laws and
previous Court decisions in the narrowest possible manner,
without running the political risk of actually overturning them.
The Court's emasculation of the Civil Rights Act of 1866 in
the *Patterson* case, for example, completely misrepresented the
aims of the Reconstruction Congress, which sought to secure
for former slaves the right to compete for advancement in the
economic marketplace. The idea that the rights of free labor
applied only at the moment of signing a contract and then disappeared would certainly have surprised them. Justice Scalia
insists that all consideration of race in legislation is barred by
the Fourteenth Amendment—a position only slightly more
extreme than that of his four colleagues—as if the framers
of that amendment viewed attempts to uplift a previously degraded group of Americans as equivalent to the discrimination
of the past.

The overall result of these decisions is to allow businesses
greater leeway in adopting employment practices that confine
minority employees to the lowest-paying jobs, and to invite endless litigation against affirmative action programs while placing
strict limits on employment discrimination suits. Each case, of
course, possesses its own set of facts and distinct litigation history. But I am less concerned here with the legal technicalities
than with what the decisions tell us about the Supreme Court
majority's social and historical vision. If Justice Marshall perhaps exaggerated in charging that the Court now views racial
discrimination as "a phenomenon of the past," the decisions
do suggest that racism is a fairly minor problem in modern

American life. This is partly because of the majority's limited definition of racism itself as fundamentally a matter of prejudiced attitudes and overtly avowed discrimination by one individual against another. The practice of "thinking by race," says Justice Scalia, is "the source of the injustice" of the past—as if racism were simply a pattern of thought and not deeply embedded in our society's economic and political institutions. The decisions explicitly disavow interest in what the Court calls "societal racism" or, at best, claim that the law provides no remedy.

To demonstrate discrimination, moreover, the Court asks plaintiffs to prove discriminatory intent. If employers do not publicly acknowledge a desire to exclude blacks (hardly a likely occurrence nowadays), even the grossest statistical disparities will not suffice. In the Alaska case, a totally segmented labor force, as well as separate company housing for white and non-white employees, was not enough to establish a prima facie case of discrimination. The plaintiffs, the Court ruled, must show the discriminatory impact of each specific company policy rather than the gross results of company actions. In *Richmond*, the fact that less than one percent of city contracts had gone to black companies in the five years before the adoption of a set-aside program proved nothing to the Court. Justice O'Connor, who wrote the majority opinion, suggested that lack of access to credit and professional training, and unfamiliarity with bidding procedures, might have limited the number of black construction contractors. It seems obvious that these "nonracial factors," as she called them, themselves stemmed from past discrimination against blacks. But O'Connor speculated that blacks might well be "disproportionately attracted to other industries than construction," as if their distribution among the occupations has always been a matter of free choice.

I do not wish to suggest that the justices in 1989 made a sudden about-face—rather, the decisions accelerate a trend, visible since the 1970s, for the Court to limit race-conscious remedies and to demand evidence of purposeful discrimination. But what *is* new, and shocking in comparing these recent decisions with those of only a few years ago, is the undisguised lack of sympathy for efforts to undo the effects of racism. The claims of white plaintiffs alleging "reverse discrimination" receive an impassioned defense, while black victims of discrimination are treated with cool reserve. In one opinion, Justice Scalia suggested that affirmative action programs were motivated by a desire to "even the score" against whites. O'Connor seems to think that the Richmond set-aside program reflects nothing more than the use of political power by a black-majority city council to "disadvantage a minority"—yet she refuses to consider that the absence of contracts to blacks in the past may reflect the previous domination of city government by whites. Even when it encounters blatant evidence of intentional discrimination, this Court fails to act. Unlike white tellers, Brenda Patterson was required to sweep the floor, was subjected to racial epithets at work, and was denied promotion, but the Court did not allow her to sue for damages.

Historians may well be struck by the ominous parallel between the reasoning of today's Court majority and that of Reconstruction's opponents over a century ago. O'Connor's statement that affirmative action programs "may in fact promote notions of racial inferiority" by making it seem that blacks must rely on government assistance to advance themselves echoes Andrew Johnson's warning that blacks wished to become wards of the state. The cry of "reverse discrimination" reminds one of Johnson's veto of the Civil Rights Bill and the

charge by other critics of Reconstruction that blacks were seeking "class legislation"—the nineteenth century's term for special privilege. To which the most effective reply was that of
black political leader William Whipper in the 1870s: "The
white race have had the benefit of class legislation ever since
the foundation of our government."

"History is irrefutable," wrote Justice Brennan in a stinging
dissent from the *Richmond* decision. And the history of slavery
and racism, embedded in the Constitution by the founding
fathers and sanctioned by law for most of our history, cannot be
erased by the sophistries of five Supreme Court justices.
Whether one believes in the jurisprudence of original intent or
in a vision of the Constitution informed by a broad understanding of our nation's past, an appreciation of history is
essential for anyone attempting to confront the continuing
racial dilemmas of our society. At its best, as Herbert Gutman
constantly reminded us, the study of history is not simply a
collection of facts, not a politically sanctioned listing of indisputable "truths," but an ongoing means of collective self-
discovery about the nature of our society. Unless the Supreme
Court learns that history, it is not likely that we shall soon see
what Frederick Douglass called for a century ago—a Court
"which shall be as true, as vigilant, as active, and exacting in
maintaining laws enacted for the protection of human rights, as
in other days was that Court for the destruction of human
rights."

NINE

KEN BURNS AND
THE ROMANCE
OF REUNION

❧

The Civil War, Ken Burns's multihour television documentary, was certainly the most successful presentation of history for a broad popular audience during the 1990s. Attracting a viewership far in excess of the usual public television audience, featured on the covers of *Newsweek* and *Entertainment Weekly,* the series combined Burns's talent as a storyteller and cinematographer with a compelling use of first-person documents that helped bring history alive. Given the tremendous interest in history inspired by the series, it seems churlish to raise objections to Burns's take on his subject.

Nonetheless, the series did have significant weaknesses as history. When the historian Robert Toplin, himself an experienced filmmaker, asked a group of scholars to comment on Burns's achievement, I chose to examine his treatment of the war's aftermath. My conclusion was that for all his cinematic talents, Burns had chosen to reinforce a vision of the war as essentially a family quarrel among white Americans, and to celebrate the road to reunion without considering the price paid for national reconciliation—the abandonment of the ideal of racial justice. Ironically, this presentation of history on the most modern of media ended up reinforcing a view of the war and its legacy that bears more resemblance to turn-of-century romantic nationalism than to modern understandings of the war's complex and ambiguous consequences.

•

In the ninth and final episode of *The Civil War*, filmmaker Ken Burns faced a daunting challenge: how to bring the war's story to a close, describe its immediate aftermath, and assess its legacy for American history. If the episode is, as I believe, the weakest of the series, it is only fair to note that Burns is not the first historian to be bedeviled by this challenge and ultimately defeated by it. Some, for instance, simply conclude their account with the surrender of Lee and the assassination of Lincoln, as though after April 1865 nothing happened. Others recognize that one cannot appraise the war's meaning or consider whether its accomplishments justified the enormous loss of life without examining the years immediately following the Confederacy's defeat and the long road to reunion that stretched into the new century. The postwar years, however, lack both the drama of the battlefield and the war's easily recognizable cast of characters. Nor do they end, even for the winning side, in a blaze of glory.

The problem of "closure" is especially acute in a television series intended for a mass public. Americans have rarely expressed much interest in the Reconstruction years that followed the Civil War, the most controversial and misunderstood era in our nation's past. A survey of high school seniors recently conducted by the U.S. Department of Education reported that fewer were able to identify Reconstruction than any other event or period of American history. "What the American public always wants," William Dean Howells once remarked, "is a tragedy with a happy ending."[1] History, alas, seldom provides unambiguously festive conclusions; nor do wars neatly settle profound political and ideological issues. The more closely one looks at the aftermath of the Civil War, the more disturbing the consequences are likely to be.

Burns appears to have found the war itself far more digestible than either its origins or its consequences. Just as the opening installment raced through the prewar decades in order to get to the battles (leaving viewers with no coherent sense of what caused the conflict in the first place), so its conclusion lingers on the events of April and May 1865—the final surrender of Confederate armies, the assassination and funeral of Abraham Lincoln—getting to the postwar era only when the episode is already half over. Then it rushes through Reconstruction to dwell at length on reunions of Union and Confederate veterans, especially the famous gathering at Gettysburg in 1913 that marked the fiftieth anniversary of the Civil War's biggest battle. From the opening remarks of historians Barbara Fields and Shelby Foote that the Civil War created the modern United States to the final acknowledgment by the veterans that each side had fought nobly for its own ideals, Burns's message is clear: the chief legacy of the war was the survival and consolidation of the nation-state, and that of the postwar era the reestablishment of a sense of national unity. As historian David Blight has remarked, this combination of nostalgia and national celebration is a "most appealing" legacy, which manages to ignore all those issues that raise troubling questions about American society today.[2]

Even on Burns's favored terrain, military history, the account of the war's ending is remarkably impoverished. There is no reflection on the war as a whole and its place in the history of warfare, no effort to assess the overall impact of industrial technology on the conflict or to sum up the strategy that finally led to Northern victory. Indeed, Burns fails even to explain *why* the North triumphed on the battlefield, except to note the fact that it possessed superior resources—hardly a guarantee of victory, as history has so often demonstrated. Once he moves to the war's broader implications and consequences, he has even less to say. Issues central to the Civil War and of obvious contemporary relevance—self-determination, political democracy, race relations, the balance between force and consent in maintaining political authority—are never addressed. The abolition of slavery is never mentioned explicitly as part of the war's meaning, while the unfulfilled promise of emancipation is all but ignored as central to its aftermath. Nor is it ever suggested that the abandonment of the nation's postwar commitment to equal rights for the former slaves was the basis on which former (white) antagonists could unite in the romance of reunion. In choosing to stress the preservation of the American nation-state as the war's most enduring consequence, Burns privileges a merely national concern over the great human drama of emancipation. The result is a strangely parochial vision of the Civil War and its aftermath, and a missed opportunity to stimulate thinking about political and moral questions still central to our society.

In choosing reunion as the theme and the veteran as the emblem of this last episode, Burns magnifies weaknesses common to the series as a whole while relinquishing the strengths of earlier segments, especially the rich feeling for how individuals exist in specific times and places. The second half of the episode abandons any sense of chronology or historical context. Burns makes no attempt to convey the state of the nation at war's end in 1865, and no explanation is offered for the failure to guarantee the equal rights of the former slaves. The photographs and newsreel footage recording the veterans' reunions are presented without regard to time or place and even on occasion without proper identification—as though the events themselves took place in a historical vacuum. A mention of the Ku Klux Klan during Reconstruction, for example, is illustrated by a famous picture of Klansmen parading through the streets of Washington in the 1920s in their familiar white robes and hoods, even though this was not the disguise worn by most Reconstruction-era Klansmen. Photos of reunions from two generations afterward accompany narration about 1865. After the detailed attention to historical chronology in previous episodes, where battles were examined day by day, even hour by hour, such complete disregard for historical sequence (to say nothing of historical causation) is profoundly disturbing.

Anecdotes and snippets of information about individual lives dominate the entire series, reducing, in good television fashion, the political to the personal. In the final episode, however, bereft of the rich texture of the earlier segments, they lose all historical meaning, not merely verging on the sentimental but, in the endless dwelling on Lincoln's funeral and the recurring images of aged veterans, becoming out-and-out mawkish.

Throughout the series, Burns focuses on specific personalities—soldiers, statesmen, loved ones on the home front—to
humanize the story of the war and bring its protagonists to
life through their often-eloquent letters and speeches. The
final episode spends much time tracing what happened after
the war to these personalities, who include military leaders such
as William T. Sherman and Nathan B. Forrest, along with figures like Mary Todd Lincoln and Alexander H. Stephens. But
in the absence of any historical framework in which to place
these stories, their significance is lost. General Philip Sheridan,
we are told, ended up fighting Indians in the West, and Elisha
Hunt Rhodes prospered in textile manufacturing. But these and
other statements exist as disembodied "facts," divorced from
the political, economic, and other contexts that give them
meaning.

Given that Burns has little interest in the legacy of emancipation, it is not surprising that of the twenty-eight persons (by
my count) whose postwar careers are mentioned, only Frederick Douglass and Hiram Revels are black. Evidently, reunion
was predominantly a concern of whites, and black women
played no role whatever in the history of post–Civil War America. Douglass, we are simply told, continued his advocacy of
civil rights. Revels, elected in 1870 from Mississippi as the first
black member of the U.S. Senate, is introduced simply as an
oddity, a foil to underscore the humiliation of Jefferson Davis
and the South, since he took the seat once held by the Confederate president. There is no effort to explain who Revels was,
how or why he became the first black American to occupy
a seat in either house of Congress, what was the larger significance of his election, or what happened to him after his
term in office.

Revels could have provided an interesting point of entry into the Reconstruction era.[3] For the record, he was one of well over one thousand black men who held public office during the decade known to historians as Radical Reconstruction (1867–77). Their advent symbolized the revolution in American life wrought by Union victory in the Civil War and the destruction of slavery. Reconstruction was a time of intense conflict over the implications of the North's triumph, in which former slaves sought to give meaning to the freedom they had so recently acquired. In demanding an end to the myriad injustices of slavery, incorporation as equal citizens into the political order, autonomy in their personal and religious lives, access to education, and land of their own, African-Americans helped to establish the political and social agenda of this dramatic period.

In 1865 and 1866, Lincoln's successor Andrew Johnson became locked in a bitter dispute with Congress. Johnson's policy of giving the white South a free hand in shaping the region's future was challenged by a Republican Congress that rewrote federal law and the Constitution to guarantee their own vision of the war's legacy. In civil rights legislation and in the Thirteenth, Fourteenth, and Fifteenth Amendments, Congress announced its commitment to equality before the law, regardless of race, as the definition of American citizenship, and it declared the national state to be the protector of the fundamental rights of all Americans. Although primarily conceived for the purpose of protecting and enfranchising blacks, these measures are not simply a concern of African-American history; rather, they are essential to an understanding of the war's legacy.

The decision in 1867 to award black men in the South the right to vote repudiated the prewar tradition that America was a "white man's government" and inaugurated the nation's first experiment in interracial democracy. Even if the new governments that came to power throughout the South were sometimes marred by corruption, they implemented numerous changes in Southern life that were forward-looking and progressive—establishing the region's first public school systems, attempting to rebuild its shattered economy, and passing laws to guarantee the equal civil and political rights of black Americans. These policies inspired a wave of opposition from the majority of white Southerners, some of whom formed terrorist organizations like the Ku Klux Klan, which attacked and murdered supporters of Reconstruction in order to drive the new governments from office. In the 1870s, as the Northern commitment to Reconstruction and the ideal of racial equality waned, Democrats regained control of one Southern state after another. By 1877, Reconstruction had come to an end, and white supremacy had been restored throughout the old Confederacy. But in modern debates over the implementation of civil rights laws, the interpretation of the Fourteenth Amendment, and the nation's responsibility to ensure equal opportunity for all its citizens, Reconstruction remains a touchstone and hence a continuing force in our lives.

To this turbulent period and the issues it raises, Burns devotes exactly two minutes. The word *Reconstruction* is never mentioned, and what little information there is about the era is random and misleading. We are told, for instance, that the former slaves received "nothing but freedom," but no attempt is made to explain what the freed people understood by freedom, why the nation did not grant it to them, or what elements of freedom they did in fact acquire. Promises to the former slaves, intones the narrator, were "overlooked in the scramble for a new prosperity," a partial and ultimately meaningless summary of a bitter history of commitment and betrayal. Of Grant's presidency, we learn only that it was corrupt; unmentioned is his willingness to use the power of the federal government to suppress the Ku Klux Klan's heinous acts of violence against Southern Republicans. The Klan itself is alluded to only as part of the postwar career of General Nathan B. Forrest, the organization's most prominent founder, who, it is said, quit the Klan when it became "too violent." Accompanying this bizarre comment (which seems to imply that some violence against the former slaves was perfectly acceptable) is an image of Klansmen in full regalia marching through the streets of Washington a half-century later. The visual impression is of a social club clothed in white robes, not a band of violent criminals.

Even when accurate, the "facts" about Reconstruction have next to no historical meaning because they exist outside any historical context. We are told, for instance, that Mississippi spent fully one-fifth of its 1865 budget on artificial limbs for former soldiers. But the significance of this "fact" is rather more complicated than Burns seems to appreciate. Mississippi's first postwar government was elected by and for whites, and the limbs were for Confederate victims alone, their purchase authorized by the same legislature that enacted the infamous Black Code that sought to reduce the former slaves to a status reminiscent of slavery. Tens of thousands of black Mississippians had fought in the Union Army, but like all African-Americans, they did not form part of the community served by the new government. Had Mississippi provided artificial limbs for *all* veterans who needed them, the cost would have been higher still. On the other hand, since Mississippi's planters were essentially unwilling to tax themselves (a large proportion of state revenue came from head taxes on individuals, regardless of income, rather than on the value of land), the state budget was extremely low, making the figure of one-fifth perhaps less impressive than appears at first glance. Had the Mississippi legislature taken seriously its responsibilities, had it raised money, for example, to provide public education for the state's children, the percentage of the budget allocated to artificial limbs would have been substantially less. My point is not that Burns should have explored all these issues in depth, simply that this particular item of expenditure, offered as a sentimental reminder of the war's human cost, might as easily have been used to illustrate the quality of postwar "reconciliation" and the ways white Southerners, returned to power by Andrew Johnson, defined the parameters of black freedom and the social responsibilities of government. This, however, would have required the filmmaker to take an interest in the struggle in postwar America to define the consequences of emancipation.

The decision to ignore Reconstruction is especially unfortunate because treating the era in greater depth would have given meaning to Barbara Fields's remark that the Civil War has not yet ended. The postwar story of Reconstruction and its overthrow, of the making and waning of a national commitment to equality, drives the point home by suggesting the historical origins of modern racial problems, thus connecting the past with the present. Instead, as so often in the series, Fields's trenchant remark becomes not the inspiration for an investigation of history but a substitute for it. Her comment is treated as a "sound bite," and as with so many others, its impact is undercut by the visual images that accompany it—in this case, newsreels of the 1913 and 1938 Gettysburg reunions. Faced with a choice between historical illumination and nostalgia, Burns consistently opts for nostalgia.

Like Alexandra Ripley, whose novel *Scarlett* has the heroine of *Gone With the Wind* implausibly wait out the Reconstruction era in Ireland, Burns chooses to ignore the contentious history of post–Civil War America. One cannot ascribe this omission to the absence of compelling visual images and first-person testimonies of the sort used elsewhere in the series. The same libraries and archives that contain the thousands of Civil War photographs Burns utilized to such telling effect in earlier episodes also possess dramatic photographs and engravings of former slaves, Klansmen, and scenes on postwar plantations. The poignancy of the letters and diaries that gave such immediacy to other parts of the series are equaled or exceeded by the moving letters, petitions, and statements before congressional committees by freed people and by white Southerners responding to the profound changes wrought by the Civil War. It is a failure of historical imagination, not the absence of historical material suitable for television, that explains the structure and subject matter of the final episode.

Let me make myself perfectly clear. The issue here is not primarily one of "coverage" but of interpretation. Ignoring the actual history of postwar America (which necessarily distorts understanding of the war itself) arises inevitably from a vision of the Civil War as a family quarrel among whites, whose fundamental accomplishment was the preservation of the Union and in which the destruction of slavery was a side issue and African-Americans little more than a problem confronting white society. Even on its own terms, however, the treatment of "reunion" is wholly inadequate, for Burns does not appear to realize that the process involved far more than simply reknitting the shattered bonds of nationhood.

If the Civil War created the modern American nation, the specific character that reunion took helped to define what kind of nation America was to be. Reunion represented a substantial retreat from the Reconstruction ideal of color-blind citizenship. The road to reunion was paved with the broken dreams of black Americans, and the betrayal of those dreams was indispensable to the process of reunion as it actually took place. This was why Frederick Douglass fought in the 1870s and 1880s not only for civil rights, as the final episode mentions, but to remind Americans of the war's causes and meaning. Douglass dreaded the implications of reunion, if it simply amounted to "peace among the whites."[4] Yet Burns seems unable to understand reunion in any other way.

Reunion took place not in a vacuum but in a specific historical context, marked by the rise of a xenophobic patriotism "imagining" the reunited nation via the language of racial exclusiveness. By ignoring this context (which included the disenfranchisement and segregation of blacks in the South, the exclusion by federal statute of Chinese immigrants, and the emergence of the United States as an overseas imperial power in the Spanish-American War), Burns surrenders the possibility of probing the costs of reunion as well as its benefits. Is it not worthy of note that 1913 witnessed not only the Gettysburg commemoration but Woodrow Wilson's order segregating federal offices in Washington, D.C.? In treating reconciliation as a straightforward, unproblematic historical process, Burns misses a golden opportunity to explore the ways reunion was linked to a specific definition of the national purpose and character, and a particular understanding of the meaning of the Civil War.

For years, historians have been aware that historical memory is unavoidably selective and that historical traditions are "invented" and manipulated. Forgetting some aspects of the past is as much a part of historical understanding as remembering others. Selective readings of the past, often institutionalized in rituals like veterans' reunions and publicly constructed monuments, help give citizens a shared sense of national identity. In the case of the Civil War, reunion was predicated on a particular interpretation of the conflict's causes and legacy. On the road to reunion, the war was "remembered" not as the crisis of a nation divided by antagonistic labor systems and political and social ideologies, but as a tragic conflict within the American family, whose great bloodshed was in many ways meaningless but that accomplished the essential task of solidifying a united nation. Its purpose, in other words, was preservation, not transformation. Both sides, in this view, were composed of brave men fighting for noble principles (Union in the case of the North, self-determination on the part of the South)—a vision exemplified by the late-nineteenth-century cult of Lincoln and Lee, each representing the noblest features of his society and each a figure on whom Americans of all regions could look back with pride. In this story, the war's legacy lay essentially in the soldiers themselves, their valor and ultimate reconciliation, not in any ideological causes or purposes. The struggle against slavery was a minor feature of the war, and the abolition of slavery worthy of note essentially for removing a cause of dissension among white Americans.[5]

This view of the war was popularized at the very veterans' reunions on which Burns dwells so extensively, where black veterans were nearly invisible (as they are in the final episode). It was reflected in the hundreds of Civil War monuments that, with only two or three exceptions, fail to include a single representation of a black soldier. It was given scholarly expression in the work of turn-of-the-century "nationalist" historians like James Ford Rhodes and Edward B. McMaster, and it was popularized for a mass audience in D. W. Griffith's *Birth of a Nation*, a cinematic paean to national unity and white supremacy that received its premiere at Woodrow Wilson's White House. A particular understanding of Reconstruction, "remembered" by Griffith as a misguided attempt to raise African-Americans to a status of political and civil equality for which they were congenitally incompetent, played a central role in this story. Frank acknowledgment of the "failure" of Reconstruction and the incapacity of black Americans provided one foundation of the nation "born" after the Civil War, a point on which white Americans, North and South, could agree as part of the process of reunion. It was the complicity of scholars in legitimating this interpretation of the war and Reconstruction that led W.E.B. Du Bois to offer an irrefutable indictment of the historical profession in "The Propaganda of History," the final chapter of his great work, *Black Reconstruction in America*.[6]

This interpretation survived for decades because it accorded with deeply entrenched American political and social realities—the abrogation, with Northern acquiescence, of the Fourteenth and Fifteenth Amendments in the South, the elimination of the Republican party from Southern politics, and the widespread conviction that Southern whites knew better than Northern meddlers how to deal with their region's "race problem." Decades ago, historians abandoned this view of the Civil War era. Yet throughout the Burns series, there are disturbing echoes of this older interpretation of the war and Reconstruction. Emancipation is essentially presented as a gift by Lincoln to blacks, the role of black soldiers is given scant attention, and Reconstruction, as we have seen, is all but ignored. (In the five-hundred-page book accompanying the television series, Reconstruction is referred to a total of three times, one of which is Shelby Foote's characterization of the period as "really cruel," a reiteration of the traditional view that granting equal rights to blacks should primarily be understood as a punishment for Southern whites.)[7]

The final episode presents the veterans' reunions as moments of "brotherly love and affection," embodiments of the fact that Northerners and Southerners (at least white ones) had come to recognize their common heroism and humanity. As former congressman James Symington comments, both sides "shared a common love of liberty" even though (in a homey but incoherent metaphor) they gave it "different English as it spun through their lives." In a speech during the war, Abraham Lincoln offered the best answer to this kind of sophistry:

> We all declare for liberty; but in using the same *word* we do not all mean the same *thing*. With some the word liberty may mean for each man to do as he pleases with himself, and the product of his labor; while with others the same word may mean for some men to do as they please with other men, and the product of other men's labor. Here are two, not only different, but incompatible things, called by the same name—liberty. . . . [Today] we behold the processes by which thousands are daily passing from under the yoke of bondage, hailed by some as the advance of liberty, and bewailed by others as the destruction of all liberty.[8]

Neither Symington nor the narrator quite gets around to appreciating Lincoln's point that the Southern definition of liberty rested on the power to enslave others, for this would suggest that the South fought for slavery as much as for freedom.

All in all, ignoring Reconstruction or casting it as an unfortunate era of corruption and misgovernment, and expelling blacks from the account of the war's aftermath, is less an oversight than an exercise in selective remembering not unlike that practiced by white Americans of the post–Civil War generation. Rather than subjecting it to critical analysis, Burns recapitulates the very historical understanding of the war "invented" in the 1890s as part of the glorification of the national state and the nationwide triumph of white supremacy. The final episode is not so much an account of how and why a particular understanding of the meaning of the Civil War flourished in post-Reconstruction America as an embodiment and reinforcement of that very understanding.

Since the Civil War, Americans' sense of national purpose has been intimately tied up with a selective memory of the conflict and what came after it. Accurately remembered, the events of Reconstruction place the issue of racial justice on the agenda of modern American life—but not if the history of that era and the costs paid on the road to reunion are ignored, misrepresented, or wished away.

NOTES

❧❧❧

1. MY LIFE AS A HISTORIAN

Originally published in Paul Cimbala and Robert F. Himmelberg, eds., *Historians and Race: Autobiography and the Writing of History* (Bloomington, Ind., 1996), reprinted courtesy of the Indiana University Press. The essay has been slightly updated.

2. THE EDUCATION OF RICHARD HOFSTADTER

Introduction to *Social Darwinism in American Thought* (Beacon Press, 1992); reprinted by permission of Beacon Press, Boston. I wish to thank Jack D. Foner, Beatrice Kevitt Hofstadter, Walter P. Metzger, James P. Shenton, Fred Siegel, and Arthur W. Wang for their helpful comments and suggestions.

1. Richard Hofstadter, "The Great Depression and American History: A Personal Footnote," typescript of lecture, Box 36, Richard Hofstadter Papers, Rare Book and Manuscript Library, Columbia University. This lecture is undated, but internal evidence indicates that it was written in the mid-1960s.
2. Alfred Kazin, *New York Jew* (New York, 1978), 15. Susan S. Baker, *Radical Beginnings: Richard Hofstadter and the 1930s* (Westport, Conn.,

1985), is the best account of Hofstadter's early career and his involvement with political radicalism.

3. Hofstadter to Kenneth Stampp, December 1944, quoted in Baker, *Radical Beginnings,* 180.

4. Hofstadter to Harvey Swados, January 20, April 30, 1938, Harvey Swados Papers, Archives, University of Massachusetts, Amherst.

5. Hofstadter to Harvey Swados, May 29, 1938, February 16, 1939, Swados Papers.

6. Hofstadter to Harvey Swados, October 9, 1939, March 1940, Swados Papers.

7. Hofstadter to Harvey Swados, October 9, 1939, Swados Papers.

8. Richard Hofstadter, "The Southeastern Cotton Tenants under the AAA, 1933–1935," unpublished master's thesis, Columbia University, 1938.

9. David Hawke, "Interview: Richard Hofstadter," *History* 3 (1960), 141.

10. Richard Hofstadter, "The Tariff Issue on the Eve of the Civil War," *American Historical Review* 44 (October 1938), 50–55.

11. Felice Swados Hofstadter to Harvey Swados, February 6, 1939, Swados Papers.

12. Hofstadter to Harvey Swados, April 15, 1939; Felice Swados Hofstadter to Harvey Swados, May 6, 1940, Swados Papers.

13. Hofstadter to Harvey Swados, May 1941, Swados Papers.

14. Felice Swados Hofstadter to Harvey Swados, June 2, 1940, with marginal comments by Richard Hofstadter, Swados Papers; Hofstadter, "The Great Depression and American History."

15. Richard Hofstadter, "Darwinism and Western Thought," in *Darwin, Marx, and Wagner,* edited by Henry L. Paine (Columbus, Ohio, 1962), 60–61.

16. Hawke, "Interview," 138. In an "Author's Note" to the 1955 edition, Hofstadter credited his second wife, Beatrice Kevitt Hofstadter, for "shar[ing] equally with me in the task of revision."

17. Irvin G. Wyllie, "Social Darwinism and the Businessman," *Proceedings of the American Philosophical Society* 103 (October 1959), 629–35.

18. Robert C. Bannister, *Social Darwinism: Science and Myth in Anglo-American Social Thought,* rev. ed. (Philadelphia, 1988).

19. Bannister, *Social Darwinism,* xviii.

20. Dorothy Ross, *The Origins of American Social Science* (New York, 1991),

85–91; Carl N. Degler, *In Search of Human Nature: The Fall and Revival of Darwinism in American Social Thought* (New York, 1991), 11.

21. Ross makes this point in *Origins of American Social Science*, as does John L. Recchiuti in "Intellectuals and Progressivism: New York's Social Scientific Community 1880–1917," unpublished Ph.D. diss., Columbia University, 1991. See also Nancy L. Stepan, "Race and Gender: The Role of Analogy in Science," *ISIS* 77 (1986), 261–77.

22. See Degler, *In Search of Human Nature*.

23. For more detailed surveys of Hofstadter's subsequent career as a historian, see Stanley Elkins and Eric McKitrick, "Richard Hofstadter: A Progress," in *The Hofstadter Aegis: A Memorial*, edited by Elkins and McKitrick (New York, 1974), 300–67, and Daniel J. Singal, "Beyond Consensus: Richard Hofstadter and American Historiography," *American Historical Review* 89 (October 1984), 976–1004.

24. Arthur M. Schlesinger, Jr., "Richard Hofstadter," in *Pastmasters*, edited by Robin W. Winks (New York, 1969), 289; Hofstadter's marginal comments on the draft of Schlesinger's essay are in the Hofstadter Papers.

25. Peter Novick, *That Noble Dream: The "Objectivity Question" and the American Historical Profession* (New York, 1988), 334n.

26. Hofstadter, "The Great Depression and American History."

27. Novick, *That Noble Dream*, 323.

28. Singal, "Beyond Consensus," 996n; Novick, *That Noble Dream*, 326.

29. Richard Hofstadter, *The Age of Reform* (New York, 1955), 14; Hofstadter to Harvey Swados, June 3, 1962, Swados Papers.

3. AMERICAN FREEDOM IN A GLOBAL AGE

Originally published in *American Historical Review* 106 (February 2001), 1–16. Reprinted by permission of the American Historical Association. Thanks to Professor Thomas Bender of New York University for inviting me to participate in the 1999 La Pietra Conference on Internationalizing the Study of American History, where some of the ideas in this essay were first developed, and for his extremely helpful comments on the paper I delivered there. I also wish to thank my colleague Victoria DeGrazia for sharing with me some of her insights on the consequences of globalization.

1. Brooks Adams, *The New Empire* (New York, 1902), 208.

2. W. T. Stead, *The Americanisation of the World: or, The Trend of the Twentieth Century* (London, 1902), 5, 59, 123.
3. David Reynolds, *One World Divisible: A Global History Since 1945* (New York, 2000), 650–51; Anthony D. Smith, *Nations and Nationalism in a Global Era* (Cambridge, 1995), 1–4; David Held et al., *Global Transformations: Politics, Economics and Culture* (Cambridge, 1999), 3–7; "Multiple Modernities," special issue of *Daedalus* (Winter 2000).
4. Karl Marx and Frederick Engels, *The Communist Manifesto: A Modern Edition* (New York, 1998), 39. See also Kevin H. O'Rourke and Jeffrey G. Williamson, *When Did Globalization Begin?*, National Bureau of Economic Research Working Paper 7633 (Cambridge, 2000).
5. Geoffrey Barraclough, "The Larger View of History," *Times Literary Supplement*, January 6, 1956, ii.
6. W.E.B. Du Bois, *Black Reconstruction in America* (New York, 1935), 15; Herbert E. Bolton, *Wider Horizons of American History* (New York, 1939), 2.
7. J. H. Elliott, *Do the Americas Have a Common History?* (Providence, 1998); Bonnie S. Anderson, *Joyous Greetings: The First International Women's Movement, 1830–1860* (New York, 2000); Matthew F. Jacobson, *Barbarian Virtues: The United States Encounters Foreign Peoples at Home and Abroad, 1876–1917* (New York, 2000); Daniel T. Rodgers, *Atlantic Crossings: Social Politics in a Progressive Age* (Cambridge, Mass., 1998); Oscar V. Campomanes, "New Formations of Asian American Studies and the Question of U.S. Imperialism," *Positions* 5 (Fall 1997), 523–50.
8. Akira Iriye, "The Internationalization of History," *American Historical Review* 94 (February 1989), 1–10. See also Lawrence Veysey, "The Autonomy of American History Reconsidered," *American Quarterly* 31 (Fall 1979), 455–77; Ian Tyrell, "American Exceptionalism in an Age of International History," *American Historical Review* 96 (October 1991), 1031–55; David Thelen, "Of Audiences, Borderlands, and Comparisons: Toward the Internationalization of American History," *Journal of American History* 79 (September 1992), 432–62; Thomas Bender, *The La Pietra Report: The NYU-OAH Project on Internationalizing the Study of American History* (Bloomington, Ind., 2000). Annual reports of this project and *The La Pietra Report* are available at *www.oah.org.*
9. Frantz Fanon, *The Wretched of the Earth*, translated by Constance Farrington (New York, 1963), 81.
10. Gunnar Myrdal, *An American Dilemma* (New York, 1944), 4.

11. Eric Foner, *The Story of American Freedom* (New York, 1998).
12. Rob Kroes, *If You've Seen One, You've Seen The Mall: European and American Mass Culture* (Urbana, Ill., 1996); David M. Potter, *Freedom and Its Limitations in American Life*, edited by Don E. Fehrenbacher (Stanford, 1976), 2–3; Jean Baudrillard, *America*, translated by Chris Turner (New York, 1988), 23.
13. Jack P. Greene, *The Intellectual Construction of America: Exceptionalism and Identity from 1492 to 1800* (Chapel Hill, N.C., 1993); Marilyn C. Baseler, *"Asylum for Mankind": America 1607–1800* (Ithaca, 1998), 4, 56.
14. Jan Lucassen, "The Netherlands, the Dutch, and Long-Distance Migration in the Late Sixteenth to Early Nineteenth Centuries," in *Europeans on the Move: Studies on European Migration 1500–1800*, edited by Nicholas Canny (Oxford, 1994), 153; Sue Peabody, *"There Are No Slaves in France": The Political Culture of Race and Slavery in the Ancien Régime* (New York, 1996), 3–5; Jack P. Greene, "Empire and Identity from the Glorious Revolution to the American Revolution," in *The Oxford History of the British Empire*, edited by William Roger Louis et al., 5 vols. (New York, 1998–99), 2:208; Linda Colley, *Britons: Forging the Nation, 1707–1837* (New Haven, Conn., 1992), 35, 53–55, 212.
15. Bernard Bailyn, *Ideological Origins of the American Revolution* (Cambridge, 1967), 119, 138–40; Theodore Draper, *A Struggle for Power: The American Revolution* (New York, 1996), 414.
16. John C. Rainbolt, "Americans' Initial View of Their Revolution's Significance for Other Peoples, 1776–1788," *Historian* 35 (May 1973), 421–22; John C. Fitzpatrick, ed., *The Writings of George Washington*, 39 vols. (Washington, D.C., 1931–44), 34:98; Roy F. Basler et al., eds., *The Collected Works of Abraham Lincoln*, 9 vols. (New Brunswick, N.J., 1953–55), 2:255.
17. Arthur H. Schaffer, *To Be an American: David Ramsay and the Making of the American Consciousness* (Columbia, S.C., 1991), 107–12; Dorothy Ross, "Grand Narrative in American Historical Writing: From Romance to Uncertainty," *American Historical Review* 100 (June 1995), 651–52; Joyce Appleby, Lynn Hunt, and Margaret Jacob, *Telling the Truth About History* (New York, 1994), 97–112.
18. Reginald Horsman, *Race and Manifest Destiny: The Origins of American Racial Anglo-Saxonism* (Cambridge, Mass., 1991), 1–4; Robert W. Tucker and David C. Hendrickson, *Empire of Liberty: The Statecraft of Thomas Jefferson* (New York, 1990).

19. Donald R. Hickey, "America's Response to the Slave Revolt in Haiti, 1791–1806," *Journal of the Early Republic* 2 (Winter 1982), 368–73; Winthrop D. Jordan, *White Over Black: American Attitudes Toward the Negro 1550–1812* (Chapel Hill, N.C., 1968), 412–14.
20. C. Peter Ripley et al., eds., *The Black Abolitionist Papers*, 5 vols. (Chapel Hill, N.C., 1985–93), 4:248–49.
21. John R. McKivigan and Jason H. Silverman, "Monarchial Liberty and Republican Slavery: West Indian Emancipation Celebrations in Upstate New York and Canada West," *Afro-Americans in New York Life and History* 10 (January 1986), 10–12; Paul Goodman, *Of One Blood: Abolitionism and the Origins of Racial Equality* (Berkeley, Calif., 1998), 235.
22. Colley, *Britons*, 351–59; James Bryce, *The American Commonwealth*, 2 vols. (London, 1889), 2:635.
23. Jerrold S. Auerbach, *Labor and Liberty: The LaFollette Committee and the New Deal* (Indianapolis, 1966), 210–13; Michael J. Klarman, "Rethinking the Civil Rights and Civil Liberties Revolutions," *Virginia Law Review* 82 (February 1996), 43.
24. Michael Kammen, *A Machine That Would Go of Itself: The Constitution in American Culture* (New York, 1987), 336; Samuel I. Rosenman, ed., *The Public Papers and Addresses of Franklin Delano Roosevelt*, 13 vols. (New York, 1938–50), 9:672.
25. Charles D. Lloyd, "American Society and Values in World War II from the Publications of the Office of War Information," Ph.D. diss., Georgetown University, 1975, 32–33; Rosenman, *Public Papers*, 10:181, 192; 11:287–88; 13:32; Mark L. Chadwin, *The Hawks of World War II* (Chapel Hill, N.C., 1966), 69–70, 275; Henry A. Wallace, *The Century of the Common Man*, edited by Russell Lord (New York, 1943), 14–19; Henry R. Luce, *The American Century* (New York, 1941), 22–27, 31–33, 37–39; John Fousek, *To Lead the Free World: American Nationalism and the Cultural Roots of the Cold War* (Chapel Hill, N.C., 2000), 73–87.
26. Wendy Wall, "'Our Enemies Within': Nazism, National Unity, and America's Wartime Discourse on Tolerance," in *Enemy Images in American History*, edited by Ragnild Fiebig–von Hase and Ursula Lehmkuhl (Providence, 1997), 210–23; Philip Gleason, *Speaking of Diversity: Language and Ethnicity in Twentieth-Century America* (Baltimore, 1992), 190–96; Lloyd, "American Society and Values," 56.

NOTES

27. Hans Kohn, *Nationalism: Its Meaning and History* (New York, 1955), 19–20; Penny Von Eschen, *Race Against Empire: Black America and Anticolonialism 1937–1957* (Ithaca, N.Y., 1997), 3.

28. Richard Pells, *The Liberal Mind in a Conservative Age: American Intellectuals in the 1940s and 1950s* (New York, 1985); Robert B. Fowler, *Believing Skeptics: American Political Intellectuals, 1945–64* (Westport, Conn., 1978); Isaiah Berlin, *Four Essays on Liberty* (New York, 1969), xliii–xlix, 118–72; Hannah Arendt, *On Revolution* (New York, 1963), 22–26, 119–21.

29. Elizabeth A. Fones-Wolf, *Selling Free Enterprise: The Business Assault on Labor and Liberalism 1945–1960* (Urbana, Ill., 1994), 1–3, 44–51; Herbert McCloskey and John Zaller, *The American Ethos: Public Attitudes Toward Capitalism and Democracy* (Cambridge, 1984), 133; *The Public Papers of the Presidents: Harry S. Truman, 1947* (Washington, D.C., 1963), 169; David F. Schmitz, *Thanks God They're on Our Side* (Chapel Hill, N.C., 1999).

30. *The Public Papers of the Presidents: Ronald Reagan, 1985* (Washington, D.C., 1988), 70; David E. Procter, *Enacting Political Culture: Rhetorical Transformations of Liberty Weekend 1986* (New York, 1991), 61–65; *The Public Papers of the Presidents: Ronald Reagan, 1986* (Washington, D.C., 1988), 1505.

31. Foner, *Story of American Freedom*, 330–32.

32. John Gray, *False Dawn: The Delusions of Global Capitalism* (New York, 1999), 216–17; Thomas L. Friedman, *The Lexus and the Olive Tree: Understanding Globalization* (New York, 1999), 309. For an alternative vision of globalization, emphasizing international social movements rather than market hegemony, see Jeremy Brecher et al., *Globalization from Below* (Cambridge, Mass., 2000).

33. Held, *Global Transformations*, 3–4.

34. Saskia Sassen, *Losing Control: Sovereignty in an Age of Globalization* (New York, 1996); John Micklethwait and Adrian Wooldridge, *A Future Perfect: The Challenge and Hidden Promise of Globalization* (London, 2000), 336–37.

35. Charles Tilly, "Globalization Threatens Labor's Rights," *International Labor and Working-Class History* 47 (Spring 1995), 4; Smith, *Nations and Nationalism*, 89, 97–98; Eric Hobsbawm, *On the Edge of the New Century* (New York, 2000), 32, 43; Michael Geyer and Charles Bright, "World History in a Global Age," *American Historical Review* 100 (October 1995), 1052–57.

36. See Jonathan Mickie and John G. Smith, eds., *Global Instability* (London, 1999).
37. Louis Hartz, *The Liberal Tradition in America* (New York, 1955), 306.

4. THE RUSSIANS WRITE A NEW HISTORY

Originally published in *Harper's*, December 1990, 70–78. Reprinted by permission of the magazine.

5. "WE MUST FORGET THE PAST": HISTORY IN THE NEW SOUTH AFRICA

Originally published in *Yale Review* 83 (April 1995), 1–17. Reprinted by permission of *Yale Review*.

6. WHY IS THERE NO SOCIALISM IN THE UNITED STATES?

Originally published in *History Workshop* 17 (Spring 1984), 57–80. Reprinted by permission of *History Workshop*.

1. Among the many reviews of the "Why is there no socialism?" debate, two of the better recent surveys are: Seymour Martin Lipset, "Why No Socialism in the United States?" in *Sources of Contemporary Radicalism*, edited by Seweryn Bialer and Sophia Sluzer (New York, 1977), 31–149, which contains an interesting section on how Marx, Engels, and other European socialists viewed the problem, and Jerome Karabel, "The Failure of American Socialism Reconsidered," *Socialist Register* (1979), 204–27. See also R. Laurence Moore, *European Socialists and the American Promised Land* (New York, 1970). An excellent collection of discussions of the history of American socialism and introduction to the Sombart question is John H. M. Laslett and Seymour M. Lipset, eds., *Failure of a Dream?: Essays in the History of American Socialism* (Garden City, N.Y., 1974). Still indispensable for the history of socialism in the United States is Donald D. Egbert and Stow Persons, eds., *Socialism and American Life*, 2 vols. (Princeton, N.J., 1952), the second volume of which consists of an exhaustive bibliography.
2. E. L. Godkin, "The Labor Crisis," *North American Review* 110 (July 1867), 177–79.

3. David Montgomery, "The Shuttle and the Cross: Weavers and Artisans in the Kensington 'Riots' of 1844," *Journal of Social History* 5 (Summer 1972); Montgomery, *Workers Control in America* (New York, 1979). James R. Green, *The World of the Worker* (New York, 1980), also stresses the predominance of "control" issues in labor struggles. An excellent recent study of the rise and fall of local labor parties in the 1880s is Leon Fink, *Workingmen's Democracy: The Knights of Labor and American Politics* (Urbana, Ill., 1983).

4. Werner Sombart's original essay has recently been printed, for the first time in its entirety, in English translation: *Why Is There No Socialism in the United States?* (White Plains, N.Y., 1976).

5. The view that the acquisition of property and high rates of geographical mobility explain the failure of socialism is expressed, for example, in Stephan Thernstrom's influential *Poverty and Progress* (Cambridge, Mass., 1964). Peter Knights, *The Plain People of Boston, 1830–1860* (New York, 1971), exemplifies a host of studies of the high rate of population turnover in nineteenth-century American cities. See also the self-congratulatory conservative version of the "success of capitalism" argument in James Nuechterlein, "Radical Historians," *Commentary*, October 1980.

6. A recent investigation, Peter Shergold, *Working-Class Life: The "American Standard" in Comparative Perspective, 1899–1913* (Pittsburgh, 1982), concludes that skilled workers in Pittsburgh did enjoy higher wages than their English counterparts but that the unskilled did not.

7. For an interesting recent example, see Ronald Schatz, "Union Pioneers: The Founders of Local Unions at General Electric and Westinghouse, 1933–37," *Journal of American History* 66 (December 1979), 586–602.

8. The idea that the West functioned as an effective safety valve for eastern labor was disproved many years ago in Carter G. Goodrich and Sol Davidson, "The Wage Earner in the Westward Movement," *Political Science Quarterly* 50 (1935), 161–85, and 51 (1936), 61–116. Quantitative methods have become far more sophisticated since then, but students of geographical mobility are still generally unable to ascertain whether men and women who moved in search of economic opportunity actually succeeded in bettering their conditions of life. The essential raw material for such studies is the manuscript census returns, using which it is easy to discover that an extremely

NOTES

high percentage of urban working-class populations had "disappeared" from one census to the next (a period of ten years). But not knowing where these individuals went, it is impossible to locate them in the next census, or to determine their occupation or wealth.

9. Louis Hartz, *The Liberal Tradition in America* (New York, 1955). The "fragment" argument is expanded in Hartz's *The Founding of New Societies* (New York, 1964). One may wonder, however, why Australia, another "bourgeois fragment" society, did give rise to a powerful labor party.

10. Richard Hofstadter, *The American Political Tradition* (New York, 1948); Daniel Boorstin, *The Genius of American Politics* (Chicago, 1953).

11. Much of this work was inspired by Herbert G. Gutman, *Work, Culture and Society in Industrializing America* (New York, 1976).

12. The "pre-bourgeois" character of the Old South is argued effectively in the works of Eugene D. Genovese. See *The Political Economy of Slavery* (New York, 1965); *The World the Slaveholders Made* (New York, 1969); and *Roll, Jordan, Roll* (New York, 1974).

13. The most significant revisionist works on the ideology of the American Revolution are J.G.A. Pocock, *The Machiavellian Moment* (Princeton, N.J., 1975), which sees republicanism extending well into the nineteenth century as an organizing paradigm of American political thought, and Gordon S. Wood, *The Creation of the American Republic, 1776–1787* (Chapel Hill, N.C., 1969), which dates the "end of classical politics" and the triumph of liberalism from the adoption of the federal Constitution in 1788. Joyce Appleby has recently sought to resurrect the idea of a dominant liberal ideology, in a more sophisticated formulation than Hartz's. See her "Commercial Farming and the 'Agrarian Myth' in the Early Republic," *Journal of American History* 68 (March 1982).

14. For the individualist strain in American radicalism, see Eric Foner, *Tom Paine and Revolutionary America* (New York, 1976); Yehoshua Arieli, *Individualism and Nationalism in American Ideology* (Cambridge, Mass., 1964); Staughton Lynd, *Intellectual Origins of American Radicalism* (New York, 1968); David DeLeon, *The American as Anarchist* (Baltimore, 1978). For the "small producer" radical ideology, see Lawrence Goodwyn, *Democratic Promise: The Populist Moment in America* (New York, 1976); Chester McA. Destler, *American Radicalism, 1865–1901* (New London, Conn., 1946). For socialist thought, see Mari Jo

Buhle, *Women and American Socialism 1870–1920* (Urbana, Ill., 1979); Nick Salvatore, *Citizen and Socialist: Eugene V. Debs* (Urbana, Ill., 1982).

15. James Weinstein, *The Corporate Ideal in the Liberal State 1900–1918* (Boston, 1968); Gabriel Kolko, *The Triumph of Conservatism* (New York, 1963). Howard Zinn, *A People's History of the United States* (New York, 1980), portrays radical movements as always being suppressed or absorbed within the liberal framework.

16. Works examining radicalism as the expression of an alternative culture include Goodwyn, *Democratic Promise;* Charles Leinenweber, "Socialists in the Streets: The New York City Socialist Party in Working Class Neighborhoods, 1908–1918," *Science and Society* 41 (Summer 1977), 152–71; and "The Origins of Left Culture in the United States: 1880–1940," a special issue of *Cultural Correspondence,* Spring 1978. The quotation is from Stanley Aronowitz, "Cracks in the Bloc: American Labor's Historic Compromise and the Present Crisis," *Social Text* 5 (Spring 1982), 45–51. See also John Alt, "Beyond Class: The Decline of Industrial Labor and Leisure," *Telos* 28 (Summer 1976), 55–80.

17. Raymond Williams, "Base and Superstructure in Marxist Cultural Theory," *New Left Review* 82 (November–December 1973), 3–16. For less sophisticated American uses of the idea of hegemony to explain the weaknesses of radicalism, see Aileen Kraditor, "American Radical Historians on Their Heritage," *Past and Present* 56 (August 1972), 136–52; Milton Cantor, *The Divided Left* (New York, 1979).

18. Richard C. Edwards, Michael Reich, and David M. Gordon, eds., *Labor Market Segmentation* (Lexington, Mass., 1975); David M. Gordon, Richard C. Edwards, and Michael Reich, *Segmented Work, Divided Workers: The Historical Transformation of Labor in the United States* (New York, 1982); Alastair Reid, "Politics and Economics in the Formation of the British Working Class: A Response to H. F. Moorhouse," *Social History* 3 (October 1978), 347–62.

19. Philip S. Foner, *Organized Labor and the Black Worker* (New York, 1974); Alexander Saxton, *The Indispensable Enemy* (Berkeley, Calif., 1971).

20. This is the argument of Mike Davis, "Why the U.S. Working Class Is Different," *New Left Review* 123 (September–October 1980), 3–46. It is also emphasized in the latest evaluation of the Sombart question, John H. M. Laslett, *Reluctant Proletarians: A Short Comparative History of American Socialism* (Westport, Conn., 1984).

21. Oscar Handlin, *Boston's Immigrants* (Cambridge, Mass., 1941); Stanley Aronowitz, *False Promises: The Shaping of American Working Class Consciousness* (New York, 1973), whose third chapter, an excellent survey of the formation of the American working class, seems to accept the notion that Catholic immigrants of peasant background are inevitably conservative; Gerald Rosenblum, *Immigrant Workers: Their Impact on American Labor Radicalism* (New York, 1973).

22. Victor Greene, *The Slavic Community on Strike* (Notre Dame, Ind., 1968); Eric Foner, "Class, Ethnicity and Radicalism in the Gilded Age: The Land League and Irish America," *Marxist Perspectives* 2 (Summer 1978), 6–55; Melvin Dubofsky, *We Shall Be All* (New York, 1969). The word *transhistorical* is taken from the important essay by Barbara J. Fields, "Ideology and Race in American History," in *Region, Race, and Reconstruction: Essays in Honor of C. Vann Woodward*, edited by J. Morgan Kousser and James M. McPherson (New York, 1982), 144. For an example of the overcoming of racism by one industrial union, see Gutman, *Work, Culture and Society*, ch. 3.

23. For another example, see Aileen Kraditor, *The Radical Persuasion, 1890–1917* (Baton Rouge, La., 1981).

24. James O'Connor, *The Fiscal Crisis of the State* (New York, 1973); Jeremy Brecher, *Strike* (San Francisco, 1972), which stresses spontaneous labor militancy, dampened by union organization itself; Philip S. Foner's multivolume *History of the Labor Movement in the United States* (New York, 1947–94), emphasizing the conservative tendencies of labor leaders, especially those of the American Federation of Labor. For the 1930s, see Schatz, "Union Pioneers," and Bert Cochran, *Labor and Communism* (Princeton, N.J., 1977), which, while unsympathetic to communist unionists, provides convincing evidence of their pivotal role in creating CIO unions. Melvyn Dubofsky questions the extent of rank-and-file militancy during the Depression in "Not So 'Turbulent Years': Another Look at the American 1930's," *Amerikstudien* 24 (1980), 12–20.

25. Selig Perlman, *A Theory of the Labor Movement* (New York, 1928), 167; Alan Dawley, *Class and Community: The Industrial Revolution in Lynn* (Cambridge, 1976), esp. ch. 8; Ira Katznelson, *City Trenches: Urban Politics and the Patterning of Class in America* (New York, 1981). David Montgomery, *Beyond Equality* (New York, 1967), also stresses how politics served as a "safety-valve" for labor discontent.

NOTES

26. For Roosevelt's flexibility, see Mike Davis, "The Barren Marriage of American Labour and the Democratic Party," *New Left Review* 124 (November–December 1980), 43–83. Alan Brinkley, *Voices of Protest* (New York, 1982), demonstrates the hold of FDR on voters otherwise attracted to radicalism. Christopher Lasch, "The Decline of Populism," in *The Agony of the American Left* (New York, 1969), is excellent on how apparent concessions to radical groups rarely involve fundamental social change. The Electoral College system, in which the party carrying a state wins the state's entire electoral vote for its presidential candidate, penalizes third parties whose strength is widely dispersed, while allowing regionally concentrated third parties to carry enough states to disrupt a presidential election by throwing the contest into the House of Representatives (as happens when no candidate receives a majority of the electoral vote).

27. A recent study of the Socialist party stressing repression is James R. Green, *Grass-Roots Socialism: Radical Movements in the Southwest 1895–1943* (Baton Rouge, La., 1978). For the first Red Scare, see William Preston, Jr., *Aliens and Dissenters: Federal Suppression of Radicals, 1903–1933* (Cambridge, Mass., 1963); for the second, David Caute, *The Great Fear* (New York, 1978).

28. Daniel Bell, *Marxian Socialism in America* (Princeton, N.J., 1967); James Weinstein, *The Decline of Socialism in America 1912–1925* (New York, 1967). Of course, every European socialist party experienced the same split between those adopting the Bolshevik model and those preferring traditional social democratic politics. See Albert S. Lindemann, *The "Red Years": European Socialism versus Bolshevism, 1919–21* (Berkeley, Calif., 1974).

29. Paul Buhle, "Debsian Socialism and the 'New Immigrant' Worker," in *Insights and Parallels,* edited by William O'Neill (Minneapolis, 1973), 249–304. John H. M. Laslett, *Labor and the Left* (New York, 1970), relates the decline of socialism in the unions. The best history of the Socialist party remains David Shannon, *The Socialist Party of America* (New York, 1955).

30. The astonishing variety of party activities comes through even in hostile accounts like Cochran, *Labor and Communism.* See also Mark Naison, *Communists in Harlem During the Depression* (Urbana, Ill., 1983), and *Radical History Review* 23 (1980), an issue devoted to the history of communist parties in Europe and the United States.

31. Davis, "The Barren Marriage"; James Weinstein, *Ambiguous Legacy: The Left in American Politics* (New York, 1975).
32. Maurice Isserman, *Which Side Were You On?* (Middletown, Conn., 1981); Nelson Lichtenstein, *Labor's War at Home: The CIO in World War II* (New York, 1982). A more sympathetic account is Roger Keeran, *The Communist Party and the Auto Workers Union* (Bloomington, Ind., 1980). See also *Radical America* 9 (July–August 1975), a special issue on American labor in the 1940s.
33. Reid, "Politics and Economics." Marianne Debouzy, "La classe ouvrière américaine: recherches et problèmes," *Mouvement social* 102 (January–March 1978), 3, notes the tendency of American historians to make unwarranted assumptions about the European working class. Perry Anderson summarizes the 1960s debates on "the whole tragedy of English labour history" in *Arguments Within English Marxism* (London, 1980), 44–46. For general problems of social democratic parties, see Adam Przeworski, "Social Democracy as a Historical Phenomenon," *New Left Review* 122 (July–August 1980), 27–58. Bruce M. Stave, ed., *Socialism and the Cities* (Port Washington, N.Y., 1975), discusses how American socialists acted in those communities where they achieved local power.
34. This was the arresting thesis of Lewis Corey, an American communist who wrote during the 1930s under the name Louis Fraina. He argued that classical socialism was a stage in the development of capitalism, a stage the United States, because of the extremely rapid expansion of capitalism in the nineteenth and twentieth centuries, in effect leaped over. In Europe, classical socialism of the Second International variety assisted the bourgeoisie in completing the bourgeois-democratic revolution, a historical task unnecessary in the United States. Harvey Klehr, "Leninism, Lewis Corey, and the Failure of American Socialism," *Labor History* 18 (Spring 1977), 249–56.

7. WHO IS AN AMERICAN?

Originally published in *Culturefront*, Winter 1995–96, 4–12. Reprinted by permission of the New York Council for the Humanities.

NOTES

8. BLACKS AND THE U.S. CONSTITUTION

Originally published in *New Left Review* 183 (September–October 1990), 63–74. Reprinted by permission of *New Left Review*.

9. KEN BURNS AND THE ROMANCE
OF REUNION

Originally published in Robert B. Toplin, ed., *Ken Burns's "The Civil War": Historians Respond* (New York, 1996). Reprinted by permission of Robert B. Toplin. Thanks to Lawrence Goldman of St. Peter's College, Oxford, and Lynn Garafola for penetrating comments on an earlier draft of this essay.

1. *Los Angeles Times,* April 3, 1990; Howells is quoted in David W. Blight, " 'What Will Peace Among the Whites Bring?': Reunion and Race in the Struggle Over the Memory of the Civil War in American Culture," *Massachusetts Review* 34 (Autumn 1993), 394–95.
2. Blight, " 'Peace Among the Whites,' " 394.
3. For the history of Reconstruction, see Eric Foner, *Reconstruction: America's Unfinished Revolution, 1863–1877* (New York, 1988).
4. Blight, " 'Peace Among the Whites,' " 396.
5. Two excellent recent studies explore the process of reunion from this vantage point: Stuart McConnell, *Glorious Contentment: The Grand Army of the Republic, 1865–1900* (Chapel Hill, N.C., 1992), and Nina Silber, *The Romance of Reunion: Northerners and the South, 1865–1900* (Chapel Hill, N.C., 1993). These works appeared after the completion of the television series, but the point about selective memory and invented traditions was readily available in earlier works, such as Eric Hobsbawm and Terrence Ranger, eds., *The Invention of Tradition* (Cambridge, 1983).
6. W.E.B. Du Bois, *Black Reconstruction in America* (New York, 1935).
7. Geoffrey C. Ward et al., *The Civil War: An Illustrated History* (New York, 1991), 273.
8. Roy F. Basler, ed., *The Collected Works of Abraham Lincoln,* 9 vols. (New Brunswick, N.J., 1953–55), 7:301–2.

INDEX

Freudianism, 42
Friedman, Thomas L., 71
Fugitive Slave Act (1850), 63, 169,
  182

Garrison, William Lloyd, 169, 174
Garrisonians, 175
Genghis Khan, 52
Genovese, Eugene D., 214*n12*
geographical mobility, 117–19
Georgian Soviet Socialist Repub-
  lic, 81, 86
Germany, 33, 86, 116, 134, 144,
  152; Nazi, *see* Nazism
Gettysburg, battle of, xiv, 191,
  198, 200
Gettysburg College, Civil War
  Institute at, 4
Gilded Age, 13, 31, 34, 37, 43
Gladiator (film), ix
glasnost, 77, 78
globalization, 49–50, 55; freedom
  and, 70–74; history of, 51–52
Godkin, E. L., 112–13
Goodrich, Carter G., 213*n8*
Gorbachev, Mikhail, 75–79, 82
Gramsci, Antonio, 125
Grand Central Terminal, x
Granger movement, 32
Grant, Madison, 162
Grant, Ulysses S., 197
Great Depression, 26, 31, 41, 80,
  119, 132, 139
Greeks, 62, 128
Green, Victor, 129
Greene, Jack P., 59
Griffith, D. W., 202
Guatemala, 5, 7

Gutman, Herbert G., 12, 13, 167,
  188

Haitians, 162
Handlin, Oscar, 128
Hartz, Louis, 40, 73, 119–23
hegemony, theory of middle-class,
  124–26
Hendricks, Thomas, 159
Herblock (Herbert Block), 181
Hiroshima, atomic bombing of,
  xii
Hispanics, 13
History Channel, The, x, xi
History Workshop, 94, 96, 103,
  108
Hitler, Adolf, 64
Hobsbawm, Eric, 11, 165, 219*n5*
Hofstadter, Beatrice Kevitt,
  206*n16*
Hofstadter, Felice Swados, 26, 27,
  29, 30
Hofstadter, Richard, xvii–xviii,
  8–9, 25–46, 120–21
Holocaust, xiii, xiv, xvii, 42
House of Representatives, U.S.,
  172, 217*n26*
Howells, William Dean, 191
Hungary, 4, 62

ideologies, historical studies of, 10,
  13, 35, 122
immigrants, 118, 127, 133, 149,
  157, 163–65, 200; eugenics
  movement and, 33; labor movement and, 127–30; limits on
  number of, 162; naturalization

Russian Revolution, 79, 84, 114
Rwanda, 101

Said, Edward, 106
Salvatore, Nick, 124
Scalia, Antonin, 181, 185–87
Schachtmanites, 27
Schlesinger, Arthur, Jr., 40
Schurz, Carl, 159
Senate, U.S., xvi, 159, 167, 194
Shenton, James P., 7
Shergold, Peter, 213n6
Sheridan, General Philip, 194
Sherman, General William
Tecumseh, 194
Shklar, Judith, 152–53
Sichone, Owen, 98
Slaughterhouse cases (1873), 183
slavery, 5–10, 13, 29, 53, 56, 57,
121–22, 141–42, 204; abolition
of, 178, 192, 195, 199, 201 (*see
also* abolitionism); citizenship
and, 152–57; Constitution and,
81, 169–77, 188; imperialism
and, 59; legacy of, 18; Library
of Congress exhibition on, 22;
and meaning of American
freedom, 61–64, 80; in South
Africa, 93; transnational movements against, 52, 62
Smith, Adam, 37
Smithsonian Institution, xii, xvi, 22
social Darwinism, 18, 25, 26,
30–40, 43, 46
social history, 11, 13, 38, 44, 94,
106, 120, 121, 149
socialism, 110–45; class consciousness and, 114–16; definitions of,

114; geographical and social
mobility and, 116–19; Hofstadter on, 28; internal errors of,
135–41; labor movement and,
127–32; liberalism and,
120–24, 143; middle-class
hegemony theory on, 124–26;
and structure of American
politics, 132–35; transnational
movements for, 52; universal
values embodied in, 79–80
Socialist parties, 144; American,
116, 122, 133, 136–40; French,
110, 114
social mobility, 117–19
Sombart, Werner, 111, 114, 116,
117, 144
South Africa, 16, 69, 88–109;
economy of, 98–99; end of
white minority rule in, xviii,
23–24, 88; higher education in,
103–6; national reconciliation
policy in, 89, 107–8; tribal and
ethnic loyalties in, 100–101
South African Museum (Cape
Town), 91
South Carolina, University of, 15
Soviet Union, 27, 68, 75–88, 140;
collapse of, xviii, 75, 110; nostalgia for czarist period in,
76–77, 83–85
Spain, xv, 58, 59, 134, 139
Spanish-American War, 33,
49–50, 160–61, 200
speech, freedom of, 56, 65
Spencer, Herbert, 31, 32, 34, 37,
39
Spooner, Lysander, 174–75
Stalin, Joseph, 78, 83, 87

Printed in the USA
CPSIA information can be obtained
at www.ICGtesting.com
LVHW091141150724
785511LV00005B/465